W9-BVU-354

11/20/07

www.sugargrove.lib.il.us

new bear

This is my old bear.

old bear

This is my small bear.

small bear

This is my big bear.

big bear

4

A Note to Educators and Parents

Learning to read is one of the most exciting and challenging things young children do. Among other skills, they are beginning to match the spoken word to print and learn directionality and print conventions.

The books in the *Our Toys* series are designed to support young readers in the earliest stages of literacy. Children will love looking at the full-color photographs while also being challenged to think about words that name objects and how those words fit into a basic sentence structure.

In addition to serving as wonderful picture books in schools, libraries, and homes, this series is specifically intended to be read within instructional small groups. The small group setting enables the teacher or other adult to provide scaffolding that will boost the reader's efforts. Children and adults alike will find these books supportive, engaging, and fun!

—Susan Nations, M.Ed.,
author, literacy coach, and consultant in literacy development

Please visit our web site at www.garethstevens.com
For a free catalog describing our list of high-quality books,
call 1-800-542-2595 (USA) or 1-800-387-3178 (Canada).
Our fax: 1-877-542-2596

Library of Congress Cataloging-in-Publication Data

Hudson, Amanda.
      This is my bear / by Amanda Hudson.
         p. cm. — (Our Toys)
      ISBN-10: 0-8368-9253-4 ISBN-13: 978-0-8368-9253-6 (lib. binding)
      ISBN-10: 0-8368-9352-2 ISBN-13: 978-0-8368-9352-6 (softcover)
      1. Teddy bears—Juvenile literature. 2. Vocabulary—Juvenile literature. I. Title.
GV1220.7.H83   2009
688.7'243—dc22   2008002028

This edition first published in 2009 by
Weekly Reader® Books
An Imprint of Gareth Stevens Publishing
1 Reader's Digest Road
Pleasantville, NY 10570-7000 USA

Senior Managing Editor: Lisa M. Herrington
Creative Director: Lisa Donovan
Electronic Production Manager: Paul Bodley, Jr.
Designer: Alexandria Davis
Cover Designer: Amelia Favazza, *Studio Montage*
Photographer: Richard Hutchings

Printed in the United States of America

1 2 3 4 5 6 7 8 9 10 09 08

This Is My Bear

3 1389 01955 4542

By Amanda Hudson

Reading Consultant: Susan Nations, M.Ed.,
author/literacy coach/consultant in literacy development

WEEKLY READER®
PUBLISHING

W9-BWH-487

CONTENTS

Santa Claus visits downtown Louisville and takes the
schoolchildren for a truck ride through the streets. Children
provided their own music with horns and noise makers.
Festivities ended with the singing of Christmas carols and
Santa throwing candy to the children. This was an annual
event sponsored by businessmen during World War I.
Louisville Public Library Collection

PREFACE

Come with us on an exciting adventure through the yesteryears of Stark County history. After the glacier melted and before the white man made his way here, this area was inhabited by Indians. A treaty with the various tribes allowed it to be surveyed in 1799 and then settled. Some Iroquois and Delawares continued to have peace talks and powwows at what became Congress Lake, Sippo Lake, and Meyers Lake as they roamed between the Tuscarawas River and Lake Erie.

The early settlers found an abundance of timber and animals, riverlets and lakes that ran clear and deep, and rolling terrain with fertile soil. The early maps show this part of Ohio as one of the Congress Lands which were opened by the government for development. Portions could be purchased, some as cheaply as $2.00 per acre, from Land Grant offices at either Lisbon or Steubenville.

The Indian tales together with early industrial successes, the founding of solid churches and schools, and interesting presidential history make the heritage of Stark County a fascinating study. That, combined with the tradition of medical and cultural advancement, as well as creative land uses, makes this area outstanding in the overall history of Ohio.

The development of the county can be traced through several periods: founding, growth, the industrial age, and the suburban era. Although periods such as these are loosely defined and perhaps somewhat arbitrary, examining the main characteristics of each can help to reveal the overall patterns of development in Stark County and allow these developments to be related to the nation as a whole.

The reader will find in this book an overview of Stark County history and a variety of images, both sketches and photographs, which again prove that a picture truly does reflect a thousand words. This volume is intended for the reader's pleasure and education.

Alliance High School's second football team in 1896. Alliance Historical Society Collection

ACKNOWLEDGMENTS

Upon embarking on this mission, *The Repository* had one goal: to call our readers to action. We asked them to dig through their attics, research their basements, and dust off their old mantel photos—and dig they did.

The outcome was many wonderful, never-seen-before glimpses of the past from cherished memories of many a Stark Countian. The response was overwhelming. The task of researching the private submissions and then researching our historical reference points to compile a unique book was more laborious than ever imagined, but the hard work paid off in this alluring visual study of our county.

Our thanks goes to several local historians, volunteers, and interested parties who took this project on with a fervor. Special thanks goes to Ruth H. Basner, local historian and author. It was with her guidance, knowledge, and deep love of history that the book took shape. Thanks also to her wonderful support staff; Craig Bara who spent day after day drawing upon the many resources all over Stark County researching for accuracy. Michele Gorton lent her typing skills and Craig James his photographic expertise. Dr. James Brandau, Joyce and David Greek, and Jack Hinton meticulously proofread the manuscript. Our thanks go to others who lent their professional expertise; Al Albacete, Carl Harsh, Jeff Brown, and others who crossed our path on a weekly basis, and lastly, to Editor William Hopper, of *The Repository's* editorial page, for his insight and knowledge of the written word which guided this tremendous undertaking along.

We would also like to thank our many readers who participated by sending submissions. Many were used, but several were returned due to space restrictions.

It is *The Repository's* hope that all who look through *Yesteryears* pages give them a true appreciation of Stark County's rich heritage.

Paula S. Mastroianni

Marketing Director and *Yesteryears* Coordinator,

The Repository

This 1923 view shows the Cable Company, an excavating, grading, and steam shovel works, preparing to excavate and develop six hundred and forty acres of land. Two hundred and fifty acres are under water today, known as Lake Cable, located halfway between Canton and Massillon. Dunlap Collection

According to early newspaper reports, this is the John Bowers cabin in Nimishillen Township. Built in the spring of 1806, it was located near Elysian Park in an orchard on a hill west of old Nimishillen Creek. John Bowers became a county commissioner and tax collector who passed from house to house in the county with a cylindrical tin box strapped over his shoulder.

A son of the Bowers was stricken with a fever the first winter after their arrival and died. A crude coffin was constructed out of an old wagon box and the boy was buried in the woods near the cabin and a tree was cut down and laid across the grave to protect it from the wolves. Louisville Public Library Collection

YEARS IN THE WILDERNESS

1805-1820

Breaking the Wilderness

I hear the tread of pioneers,

Of nations yet to be;

The first low wash of waves

Where soon shall roll a human sea!

The elements of empire here

Are plastic yet, and warm;

The chaos of a mighty world

Is rounding into form!

What heroism, what perils, then!

How true of heart and strong of hand,

How earnest, resolute, these pioneer men!

—1875 Atlas

Stark County, which lies in the northeast quadrant of the state, was originally part of Columbiana County. It was organized by the Ohio State Legislature on March 16, 1809, just six years after Ohio was admitted to the Union as the seventeenth state. Four villages—Canton in 1805, Osnaburg and Bethlehem in 1806, and Lexington in 1807—predate the establishment of Stark County, and seven more were founded in the next seven years. This rapid growth was followed by a ten-year break before more villages were recorded.

Stark County's founding and settlement were a part of the great westward movement in the United States during the nineteenth century. The county was named for distinguished

This sketch shows the first building of the *Ohio Repository* located on Market Street, South, built by John Saxton in 1817. *Repository* Files

Right: Ellis N. Johnson, founder of the village of Mount Union, was born April 1, 1789, and died September 15, 1889. This picture was taken on the hundredth anniversary of his birth. The father of sixteen children, he was affectionately known as Uncle Ellis. Johnson was prominent in the antislavery movement and was involved in the Underground Railroad. He was a personal friend of John Brown and William Henry Harrison. Johnson was a Stark County Justice of the Peace for twenty-three years and served two terms as mayor of Mount Union. Alliance Historical Society Collection. Mount Union College

Boyhood home of John Stark, Manchester (also known as Londonderry) New Hampshire. Heritage Information Center Collection

Revolutionary War General John Stark whose reputation was carried by many Revolutionary War veterans to Ohio. He and his wife Molly were never west of Buffalo, New York. They were parents of ten children, one of whom, Caleb, owned land in Tuscarawas County and southern Ohio. In 1929, when a tuberculosis sanitarium was built near Alliance, it was named Molly Stark Hospital in honor of the General's wife, who often nursed sick and wounded troops in their home in New Hampshire.

Those who first settled here were white families that had traveled over the mountains from eastern Pennsylvania in their Conestoga wagons. The trip often took several seasons. These families spoke what became known as the Pennsylvania-Dutch dialect. They generally worshipped as Lutheran, Reformed, Presbyterian, Catholic, or Methodist. In the beginning, some denominations shared a church building for worship. Many immediately built small log neighborhood schools on land allotted by the state for such purposes.

Stark County's three original major centers are Canton, Massillon, and later, Alliance. Since Canton's history dominates the Stark County story, it is featured first. It is noteworthy that its founder, Bezaleel Wells, came here with the expressed purpose of establishing a community by selling off pieces of land that he acquired from the U.S. government. Having been one of the thirty-five members of the Ohio Constitutional Convention, he had the opportunity to buy land early and cheap.

Altogether, Wells purchased about 566 square miles of land on May 14, 1805. He immediately began to apportion it and, by November, the original plat for the Village of Canton was recorded. It was designated as the county seat. There were three hundred lots in a ten-block square area that he developed as Canton. It is said that on October 22, 1806, a horse race was held at the forks of the Nimishillen, south of Canton, to help with the sale of Canton lots.

In 1814 Wells sold the courthouse site to the newly organized Stark County commissioners for $10.00 and turned over to them 150 unsold lots. Wells donated the proceeds from the sale to the commission for the construction of the first courthouse. Andrew Meyer bought 1,080 acres of land around Wells Lake in 1817 from Bezaleel and renamed it Meyers Lake. Massillon, founded November 24, 1826, was laid out by James Duncan along the Tuscarawas River. Duncan named the new village "Massillon" in honor of Rev. John Baptiste Massillon, celebrated Roman Catholic French Bishop of the court of Louis XIV. Massillon included the village of Kendal, which had been founded in 1812 by Thomas Rotch whose wife Charity established a private school for young orphans there.

The first county courthouse was completed in 1818. During the 1820s the Canton Masonic Lodge No. 69 F.&A.M. was organized and the original Presbyterian congregation was founded in Canton. Around that time, Canton's Fire Department was established.

Ohio Indian Trails in Stark County, Ohio

Typical of the early log houses is the one pictured above, which originally stood in the area between West Ely Street and West Main Street near the Keiter railroad crossing. Isaac Keiter came to live in the cabin in 1885. He was a watchman at the crossing. Three of the gentlemen are identified; at left is Isaac Keiter, in the doorway is Roy Keiter, and at right is Sam Keiter at the grinding wheel. Alliance Historical Society Collection

The early period in Stark's history can be characterized by an agricultural economy based on small farms. The most important crops were timber, apples, and wheat; Merino sheep were the most popular breed of livestock. Great sources of coal, clay, and other minerals were discovered under Stark County and would become the basis of several major industries for development in the years to come.

Unlike Canton or Massillon, the original villages of Stark County grew from prominent road crossings where early mercantile endeavors had begun such as general stores, taverns, blacksmith shops, and mills. The farming neighborhoods around them supported these crossroad centers and eventually villages grew up.

While farmers and their families worked small individual plots of land, these early years gave rise to Stark's first industries. They

General John Stark (1728–1822), was born in Londonderry, New Hampshire. Stark County was named for him although he was never west of Buffalo, New York. He served with great distinction in the Revolutionary War. Heritage Information Center Collection

Captain Mayhew Folger discovered surviving mutineers from H.M.S. *Bounty* on Pitcairn Island in 1808. He ran Kendal Tavern on State Road, near today's reservoir and he was the first toll collector at Port Massillon on the Ohio and Erie Canal. Massillon Museum Collection

were mainly related to agriculture, including gristmills and tanneries. However, potteries and farm tool inventors also began to play an important role in the formation of industry. It is important to note that during these years of carving a living from the wilderness, the first schools and churches were built, banks were organized, a library was founded, and a newspaper, *The Ohio Repository*, was established by John Saxton. It was the grandfather of today's *Repository*.

Elson Flouring Mill at Magnolia, constructed in 1834, the year Magnolia was founded. Stark County Regional Planning Files

HOMES, CHURCHES, AND THE OHIO AND ERIE CANAL

1820-1840

Stark County's geographical position between the Allegheny Mountains to the east and the Mississippi River and western Great Lakes to the west was well situated for growth. Industrial progress was exemplified by the founding of Joshua Gibbs Plow Manufacturing Company in 1836. It was followed in the next decade by the C. M. Russell Company of Massillon in 1842 and then the C. Aultman Company in 1851, all makers of farm equipment.

During the ten years between 1826 and 1836, Stark County experienced another period of growth with the founding of twenty-five new villages. The economy remained largely agricultural with a few primitive industries, but the coming of the Ohio and Erie Canal and then the railroads offered increased opportunities for trade with the outside world.

In 1825 the first stage line was run from Canton, and the Ohio and Erie Canal was begun. This waterway connected Cleveland to Portsmouth, reaching Massillon in 1828, and was finally completed in 1832. The canal brought a period of economic prosperity for Massillon, as it became the center for exportation of Stark County wheat and other goods.

In 1837 the Stark County Infirmary was built on what became North Cleveland Avenue in Canton (just north of Twenty-fifth Street). It was an enormous building which housed indigents (mostly men), situated on a large farm area, which was operated to provide food for the inmates. A barn, now located on Malone

The Freedom Tavern or American House, as it was sometimes known, was built in the mid 1830s and located at the corner of Walnut and Vine Streets in the village of Freedom (now known as Alliance). The tavern and hotel was frequented by those families traveling to the new frontier out west during the 1800s. Alliance Historical Society Collection

College Campus, is the remaining vestige of the outbuildings surrounding the home.

Stark County's economy continued to develop, but Massillon's canal boom ended in the 1850s. This was caused by the completion of the Cleveland and Pittsburgh Railroad through Alliance in 1851 and the Ohio and Pennsylvania Railroad through Canton in 1852. Like the canal, the railroad benefited Stark County farmers by providing better access to outside markets.

Mills and tanneries continued to prosper. With the coming of both the canal and the railroads, the manufacturing of farm equipment was most profitable by providing access to necessary raw materials. New industries benefited from Stark's natural resources, including coal, shale, gravel, and limestone, and the resources of other regions via the railroad. Of course, this increase of commerce brought new folks to the area to join the early

Spring Hill Farm Homestead was begun by Thomas Rotch in 1823, but he died while it was in construction. It was completed by his widow Charity Rotch who died soon after it was finished in 1824. Arvine Wales, following the death of his first wife, lived with Thomas and Charity Rotch from 1822 to 1824, first in their log cabin home and then in the new home upon its completion. Wales purchased it from the Charity Rotch Estate in 1831. Massillon Museum Collection

This 1930s view of North Park in Alliance shows some of the century homes of the day. On the right is the Philip Sharer residence. A German emigrant, he was a cabinet maker who opened his first store in the 1840s. Today the house has evolved into the Sharer-Sterling-Skivolocke Funeral Home, the community's oldest business. The house second from the right is the Foltz residence. This Virginia Quaker family settled in the area in the early 1800s. Alliance Historical Society Collection

farming families, bringing the county population to 34,603 by 1840.

The first homesteads built in this area were small, lean-to shacks. In fact, there is evidence that some farmers built their barn first and lived in it, or in a small adjoining building. As they prospered, they helped each other build more substantial houses. It was often a three-story structure with a summer kitchen in the Amish style. These families generally had four to ten children and several generations lived together, thus the need for large houses. The cooking was done on wood or coal stoves, and the water supply was an outside pump. Of course, "the necessary" was near the back door. In the villages, smaller homes were built on much smaller lots at first.

Wardrobes, including men's clothes, in those days were mostly hand-made by the mother, grandmother, or older sister. As general stores increased their inventory, "store bought" clothes became more fashionable. Household furnishings were also provided by the quick needles of pioneer women, while the men built beds, tables, and chairs out of timber from nearby woods. They also made their own wagons and buggies, which, together with the horse, were the families' main transportation. Parents made toys for the children from metal, wood, or fabric.

As soon as the first families began to arrive in the Stark County area, they established buildings for worship. Early congregations established a church at Zion Cemetery on Pittsburg Road and the Warstler Church was built at what is now Fifty-fifth Street and Middlebranch Road as early as 1814. Both buildings first served two congregations—the German Reformed and German Lutheran. Several villages organized churches around 1820. St. John the Baptist Catholic Church was founded in Canton in 1823.

The Conn House stood on the southeast corner of the Mount Union Square. John Hair built the structure in 1836 and served liquor there until the temperance league forced him to sell and leave the village. The building was sold to Mr. Conn in 1840. He operated a hotel and eating establishment there for many years. The building which is shown here in the 1880s was torn down during the later part of the Depression to make way for a gas station. Alliance Historical Society Collection

This building was constructed as a residence and Stage Coach Stop, circa 1829, in Hartville and is now occupied by the Pantry Restaurant. *Repository* **Files Collection**

In the early days, the churches were served by ministers and priests who traveled by horseback to conduct meetings at local church buildings. In some cases it was many years before congregations had resident ministers. Sunday Schools were introduced early and were shared by both congregations. Often the land for the church was donated, along with acreage for a cemetery. Sometimes a school would also be erected nearby. These were not only worship and educational centers for the rural neighborhoods, but they also served as a social meeting place. As the adults worshipped all day Sunday in church, the children would play in the schoolyard or nearby graveyard.

Another sign of lasting progress was the state legislation that created the public school system. State legislator and founder of Canton Academy, James W. Lathrop, first tried to create a school system in 1822. His legislation was commonly called Ohio's Liberal Education Act. At first it met with some opposition. However, he reintroduced the bill and was successful in 1825. It allowed for popular education at public expense and was to be administered by a State Board of Education.

The Garretson House, which stood on the northeast corner of Mount Union Square, was built in 1837 by Victor Millhouse. The building served as a home, general store, Mayor's office, post office, and restaurant before Pierce Garretson and his family moved into the building in 1846. During the family's ownership, the structure gained prominence in the abolitionists' cause. It was the stopping place for many well-known leaders of the anti-slavery cause, including Senator Charles Sumner, Lucretia Coffin Mott, and Sojourner Truth. In 1967 it was destroyed to make way for a parking lot. Alliance Historical Society

In 1831 the Village of New Berlin was founded, later to become the City of North Canton; in 1834 Louisville was established (in 1960, they both reached the population level to become cities). Reflecting the German heritage of its founders, New Berlin was so named. However, because of the same German heritage it was forced to change its name in 1918 when America was at war with Germany, as did East Canton. Louisville was originally *Lewisville* in honor of the founder's son. However, when the name was recorded in Columbus, it was found that another community was using the Lewisville name, so the spelling was changed to *Louisville*.

Although the Canal did not remain successful, it became a valuable piece of our history which we look at today with wonder and awe. The living style and fervor of religion continued to be two of the strengths of this area, which will never change.

The Conn House stood on the southeast corner of Mount Union Square. John Hair built the structure in 1836 and served liquor there until the temperance leaque forced him to sell and leave the village. The building was sold to Mr. Conn in 1840. He operated a hotel and eating establish-ment there for many years. The building which is shown here in the 1880s was torn down during the latter part of the depression to make way for a gas station. Alliance Historical Society Collection

Dr. Levi Leslie Lamborn (right), a political foe and personal friend of William McKinley, built this house in Alliance in 1857. Lamborn will be remembered for pioneering the development of the carnation in the United States. Just before his debates with McKinley, Lamborn would present his opponent with his newly created scarlet carnation. McKinley loved the flower and came to regard it as lucky. The sentimental association of the carnation and McKinley influenced a joint resolution of the Ohio General Assembly in 1905 selecting the scarlet carnation as our state flower. Alliance Historical Society Collection

EDUCATION, RAILROADS, AND A KILLING FROST

1840-1860

Religion and education were still important parts of the communities during the agricultural and industrial growth periods in Stark County. Education closely followed religion as a high priority. The first library had opened in 1815; private schools followed. The late 1840s saw the founding of Mount Union College and the beginning of the public school system in Canton and Massillon.

From the very beginning, there is evidence that the earliest pioneers were interested in developing good education. They themselves were not highly schooled and they wanted better instruction for their children. The first schools throughout the county were usually built on pieces of land provided by the government or on farmer-donated land. The men in the typical neighborhood would construct a one-room log building and collect money to buy books and hire a teacher. Pupils of all ages attended school. The older children helped to teach and train the younger ones. The older boys kept the pot-bellied stove, which stood in the middle of the room, fired up with logs. Boys did not attend school during the spring and autumn months due to the planting and harvesting of crops.

It should be noted that the schools were situated about two miles apart. With the land ordinance of 1785, the sixteenth section of land

The Evangelical Methodist Church at Uniontown was built in 1857–58. It later became the Town Hall, Opera House, a basket-ball court, and a comb factory, before being razed in 1935. May Parsons Collection

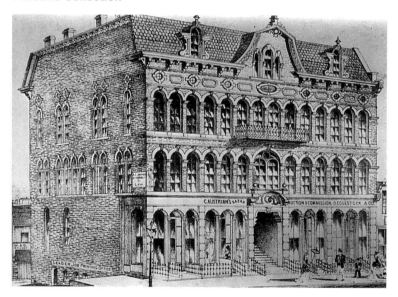

The Opera House shown in this artist's conception will be best remembered for one performance, its last. The architectural pride of Alliance was lost to the village June 2, 1886, when it crashed to the ground without warning. Miraculously enough, no one was killed although high school commencement exercises were scheduled for several days later. The collapse was attributed to faulty construction and inferior material in spite of the fact that twenty years earlier it had been built at a cost of $80,000. Alliance Historical Society Collection

The original Alliance depot was a grandiose, gondolaed affair, built on the north side of the railroad tracks. Colonel Daniel Sourbeck first opened his famous dining room in this building. The greatest railroad tragedy of Alliance occurred here when a Cleveland and Pittsburgh train crashed into an Ohio and Pennsylvania train with the cars ramming into the station house. Eleven were killed and twenty seriously hurt. Alliance Historical Society Collection

was set aside for a school building. Therefore, they were fairly close to each other. It should also be recalled that the school-age boys usually helped to find food, and they often carried their guns to school should they find some game to kill on their way to or from classes. In fact there are stories that at recess the young men made a contest of shooting objects from a nearby fence. The schoolhouses that replaced the log buildings were also one room, but larger, finished buildings. There are still some examples of these buildings throughout the county. All the villages had an education center, and schoolhouses, however rustic, dotted the countryside.

Money from the Charity Rotch Estate was used to found the Charity School in 1844 at Massillon for orphaned children. *1896 Atlas*

The female teachers who were hired in these communities had to adhere to very strict social standards. In some cases, they could not be seen in public with a man, wear lip rouge, or let their hair hang down, and they were paid a small amount. They could not let their ankles be uncovered and they usually had to keep the classroom clean. When a schoolteacher married, she had to "retire" from teaching.

In these early days of one-room schoolhouses, there were no teams to play on or cheer for, no debates to argue or listen to, no language clubs to join. But there was one competition in which many of the accomplished students took great pride—the Spell Downs. They were much like the spelling bees annually performed in today's schools, with the exception that the winners did not go beyond their own area for competition. The routine was somewhat different in that when sides were chosen one good speller would be selected as "the trapped." It was that person's responsibility to spell properly any word the rival team missed. The trapper would keep a record on a slate of the number of words properly spelled. Scoring was by counting those words spelled correctly, while misspelled words cost the team an error. It the trapper misspelled a word, two errors were counted. The winning team was the one with the least number of errors.

There was another format where everyone participating would stand. When they misspelled a word, they would have to sit down. These exercises were broken up by fifteen- or twenty-minute recesses. Since they would be held in the evening, they also became social events with refreshments and an opportunity for the young ladies to be escorted home by the young men.

Each fall there was an event which not only took care of the harvest of apples but also provided another social outlet. As the apples became ripe and the cool weather set in, each farmer would pick a day for "snitzing." This loosely translates "preparation of apples." At the appointed time, the apples would be sorted, some for pressing into cider and others for apple butter.

Those for apple butter would be pared and cooked until thick and dark. This usually took place in the great kitchens that most farmhouses had. The young men and girls of the neighborhood would help by rolling the rugs out of the way, paring the apples by hand or by patented, hand-operated, paring machines. Then the apples would be cut into sections and cooked down.

This structure was located on North Park on the original square in the Village of Freedom. Built in 1842, it was the home of Samuel Shaffer, a German emigrant who moved to Freedom from Pennsylvania. Shaffer operated a store in this house until 1851 when the Cleveland and Wellsville Railroad was completed. The house then served as the area's first railroad station.
Alliance Historical Society Collection

When the work was done such games as "Blind Man," "Hunt the Thimble," and "Love in the Dark," were played. Someone usually was handy with the fiddle, and dancing followed the games. Afterward, the young ladies were escorted home by the young gentlemen.

In 1846 a subscription school was built in the village of Mount Union. Two years later it became Mount Union Seminary. Ten years later in 1858 it became Mount Union College.

The village of Alliance came into being in 1850. It is often thought that its name, *Alliance*, came from the joining of the villages of Williamsport, Freedom, and Liberty. However, historians make it clear that it was the alliance of major railroads that gave the city its name. Mathias Hester seems to be the one responsible for the railroads coming to Alliance. He offered the community leadership and as much land as they needed to bring the magic rails to that area. The folks in Canton thought the railheads should have been there, but the C&P Railroad—then known as the Cleveland and Wellsville Railroad—was completed in 1850 when Alliance was founded. The first passenger train went

Built in 1848, the Tremont House was the center of Massillon's social, civic, and night life. It continued as a meeting place for the great and near great until 1868. It gradually declined and for four years, from 1869 to 1872, operated under different management as the Zeilly House. In 1873 it became the Sailer Cigar factory. In 1901 it changed back to the Sailer Hotel and in 1945 it became the Erie Hotel. Its demise was a spectacular fire on April 1, 1974. The remains of this historic structure were razed on December 15, 1975, and replaced with a city employee parking lot. **Massillon Museum Collection**

through on July 4, 1851. That same year the Pittsburgh, Fort Wayne, and Chicago Line was completed to Alliance. It later became the Ohio and Pennsylvania Railroad.

Twenty years later the Valley Railroad came into being. It ran from Cleveland via Akron on to Canton with stops along the way in smaller communities such as Marchand near New Berlin. It was later acquired by the Baltimore and Ohio Railroad.

Chapman Hall was designed by Simeon Porter, a prominent Ohio architect of the nineteenth century. This Romanesque style building is the only remaining Civil War–era college building designed by Porter in Ohio today. Alliance Historical Society Collection

Because of our agricultural environment, it is not surprising that the first Stark County Fair was held as early as October 15 and 16 in 1850. A large viewing stand and numerous barns and outbuildings were constructed near Meyers Lake to accommodate the displays of animals, hand-made foods, and stitchery.

Throughout Northeast Ohio in the late spring of 1859, there was great promise for a successful wheat crop. However, on the evening of June 4th and into the early morning hours of the 5th, a major disaster occurred. Many of the local farmers, feeling very confident, had borrowed heavily against the wheat crops to improve their property and buildings. The weather was remarkably fine throughout all this part of the state just as the bloom was on the wheat. An unpleasantly cool wind increased throughout Saturday the 4th; in fact, an overcoat was needed. The sky cleared in the night creating a heavy frost. Sunday morning found all the wheat and fruit had been killed. The fields were described as being "an awful sight." In a few days all the wheat fields had turned black. Some of the farmers just plowed under the destroyed crop, while others cut, then plowed, and planted fast-growing buckwheat. It was said that folks ate more buckwheat pancakes that summer than any other time in their lives. Since Northeast Ohio was the only area struck by the bitter frost, wheat was shipped in from other markets in order to keep the market price normal. In fact, wheat had never been sold so cheaply. The year of the "Great Frost" remained in the minds of many Stark County farmers for years to come.

This view of the Public Square in Canton shows the old courthouse before remodeling. William McKinley had an office in the building at the left. Stark County Historical Society Collection

THE GREAT REBELLION IN STARK COUNTY

1860-1880

The Civil War era gave the residents of Stark County another opportunity to show their patriotic fervor. Many of the original heads of families who came here early had served in the Revolutionary War. There were also many who answered the call in the War of 1812 and the Mexican War.

Throughout the county families were gathering at general stores and post offices for word of Lincoln's election. In most areas there was great celebrating when word reached the countryside from Canton that Abraham Lincoln had been elected. On the heels of his election, the "Great Rebellion" started. At the time, the war was very seldom referred to as the *Civil War*. Instead it was dubbed the *Great Rebellion* or *The War Between the States.*

Most Stark County communities welcomed the election of Lincoln. Typical of that enthusiasm, on the square of New Berlin a flagpole was placed and outfitted with a handmade flag. It was intended that each day the flag would be flown. However, when the *Stark County Democrat,* a pro-South newspaper from Canton, began to tell the other side of the story, flags few less often and local discussions became heated.

Scottish native Archibald McGregor, editor of *Stark County Democrat,* was outspoken for slavery and incorporated in his editorials views that made the local citizens question the right of the federal government to tell the states what they should or should not do on this and other issues. The result was that around the pot-bellied stove of one general store the Unionists would gather to discuss their views, and at another such gathering place the Southern Sympathizers would meet.

The Matthew Earley Home which was built in 1867 is a fine example of Italianate style architecture common in this area between 1850 and 1880. Mr. Earley was a gentleman farmer and businessman who also served many years as a city councilman. The Earleys' adopted daughter Mabel Hartzell was a founder of the Alliance Historical Society. She willed this home to them in 1954. In recent years it has been restored to its Victorian era style and is open to the public. Alliance Historical Society Collection

Right page: William McKinley during the war years of the 1860s. *Repository* Files Collection

One of the first things President Lincoln did in reaction to the firing on Fort Sumter was to ask for seventy-five thousand men to volunteer for three months to squelch the Southern uprising. To fill out the ranks, a draft was initiated. In Stark County the draft was taken to township. All able-bodied men from age eighteen to forty-five years were subject to be called. Because in some cases men of that age could not leave their families and farms, a system of substitutions was devised. A neighbor who had not been drafted could take the place of a draftee for the sum of $450.00, which was a lot of money in those days.

In the winter session of the Ohio Legislature in 1862–63, the Militia Law was enacted. This authorized military companies to be organized and armed to protect the local citizenry. They wore uniforms and held weekly drills (usually in corn fields in order to keep the lines straight) and established a ranking system. This became known as the Ohio National Guard.

The Dick Farm Machinery Company located at West Tuscarawas and Schroyer (Canton) was founded in 1874 by Joseph Dick Jr. Jesse Gingrich became president in 1924 and the firm was purchased by the Gingrich family. After a reorganization in 1930 the name changed to Blizzard Manufacturing Company. The company was liquidated in 1951.
Repository **Files Collection**

One old-timer said, "We will have war, terrible bloody war." But for several young Union ladies this was an opportunity to support the soldiers of Stark County. One might call them cheerleaders—as they donned red, white, and blue outfits complete with stars and stripes. They linked arms and paraded up and down the village pathways singing Union war songs.

As Union soldiers passed through Stark County, they were welcomed. Local residents often fed them well and even washed their clothes. Some of these units were looking for draft-dodgers who had not reported or soldiers who came home without permission. Once in a while you find a tale of a young man who maimed himself in some way to avoid the draft or played dumb and speechless when asked questions. Despite these unpatriotic few Stark Countians, scores of young men "answered the call" (more than four thousand were enrolled). Most communities today have monuments or markers dedicated to those who served in that war or were killed.

Four Stark County captains were killed in the Civil War. They were Captain James Wallace (hometown unknown), Captain

The Lake Center School at 1184 Lake Center Avenue, Uniontown, was constructed in 1863 is now owned by the Lake Board of Education. Stark County Regional Planning Files

The Methodist Church on Maple Street in Wilmot was organized in the 1860s. The deed to the church lots was dated June 30, 1866, and construction began soon after. Stark County Historical Society

First National Bank Building was built in 1866 on the corner of Tuscarawas and Market Streets in Canton. It was replaced in 1921. The Shaeffer Opera House can be seen on the right. *Repository* **Files Collection**

Bernard F. Steiner of Pike Township, Captain William Rakestraw of Washington Township, and Captain Joseph S. Harter of Canton.

> *With sad and loving hearts we come*
> *To honor those whose work was done*
> *To save our native land.*
> *When bloody war our land did fill,*
> *They left their homes with loyal will,*
> *And by our flag did stand.*

—Henry C. Holl, May 30, 1887, to commemorate Decoration Day. This is the first stanza of his fifty-four-verse poem.

Stark County resident Elizabeth Bitzer happened to be at Gettysburg when President Lincoln made his now-famous address, and she shook his hand. Elizabeth was there delivering blankets, bandages, and woolen wear to local soldiers.

William S. Lindesmith started his business in 1876. It grew from this one-room harness business to one of Alliance's most successful hardware businesses. He had the most complete and extensive harness store in this part of the state. Alliance Historical Society Collection

The Paquelet Furniture Company in Louisville is shown circa
1875. Louisville Public Library Collection

Stark County history during and after the Civil War shows major events which fashioned the next period of time. In 1863 the First National Bank of Canton was founded and in 1867 Issac Harter established a Private Bank. In 1868 a grand opera house was built in Canton (the second in Ohio) and Massillon was incorporated as a city. In 1870 the second Stark County Courthouse was dedicated.

Two well-known manufacturers moved here in 1871 and 1872. Morgan Engineering came from Pittsburgh and Diebold Safe and Lock Company moved from Cincinnati. The Hoover family also transferred their tanning business from the farm into New Berlin in 1875. They began making a complete line of leather horse-gear, hiring ten people and one office clerk. At about this same time Canton Business College opened (1876) and *The Repository* began daily publication (1878). These were true signs Stark County was progressing.

This March 1867 view shows East Tuscarawas from Market Avenue. The building is being moved to make way for George D. Harter's first bank building. *Repository* **Files Collection**

Robert A. Pinn was one of four blacks to win the Congres-sional Medal of Honor in the Civil War. He was admitted to the bar as a U.S. pension attorney in 1879. Stow armory was named for him—the first ONG armory named for a black. Massillon Museum Collection

This woodcut shows the Aultman reaper as advertised in 1872. *Repository* Files Collection

An early artist's conception of the famous Sourbeck House, also known as the Pennsylvania Railroad Station, located at the end of East Main Street in Alliance. It was known for its excellent cuisine and the famous figures who stopped there. Twenty-five large bedrooms occupied the top floor as well as a large parlor for the lady guests. The three principal generals on the Union side of the Civil War—Grant, Sherman, and Sheridan—once dined together at the Sourbeck House. Alliance Historical Society Collection

1875 Atlas

1875 Atlas

STARK COUNTY
DEMOCRAT BUILDIN

JOB PRINTIN

26 A. McGREGOR & SON.

Fairmount Children's Home is shown in the 1880s. In 1847 an act was passed by the state legislature authorizing counties to combine for the formation of children's home districts. Following the Civil War, hundreds of Ohio children were left homeless. The commissioners of Stark, Carroll, Columbiana, Jefferson, and Mahoning Counties met at Salem, June 25, 1874, for preliminary discussion. Out of this grew the Stark-Columbiana Children's Home District which was authorized February 18, 1875, to issue bonds for the 153 acres of land 3-1/2 miles south of Alliance. The administration building shown in this picture was completed and dedicated in October 1876. Subsequently five cottages, a school chapel, detention home, laundry, and other buildings were added. The home closed in 1976. Stark County Historical Society

1875 Atlas

Canal Fulton Jail House. Canal Fulton Heritage Society Collection

The Canal Fulton–Sullivan House was built in 1879 and now is a public library. Canal Fulton Heritage Society Collection

Charles Alva Lane, founder of the Hillgreen and Lane Pipe Organ
Company, built this house on South Union Avenue in Alliance in
the late 1860s. It was purchased by Mount Union College where
it served as the presidents' residence and the Conservatory of
Music. Shown here around 1890, it was torn down in the 1960s.
Craig Bara Collection

The Massillon Opera House was constructed in 1869 and was considered to be the finest between Pittsburgh and Chicago. In 1929 the third floor was removed and the building was torn down in 1966 to make way for a parking lot. Massillon Museum Collection

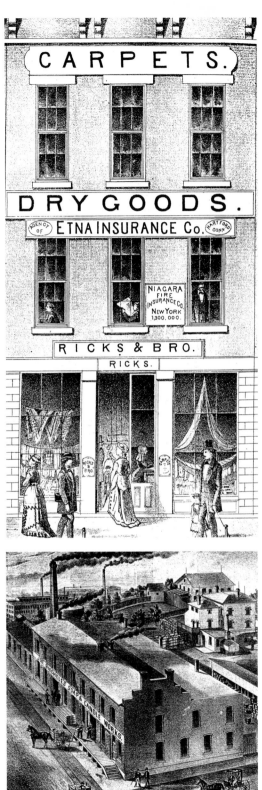

1875 Atlas

ﾞe townspeople have gathered in the Alliance public square in April 1873 to
ﾟdicate the newly purchased pumper engine and the new water pump which
ﾟas built over a large cistern used for fire fighting purposes. Alliance
ﾟstorical Society Collection

ﾟft: For many years Mr. and Mrs. Harrison Judd operated a rooming and
ﾟarding establishment for students at Mount Union College. Built in 1872
ﾟbecame a favorite student "hangout." In addition to the fine cooking, Mrs.
ﾟdd was sought out by students for her advice and counsel. The building
ﾟas acquired by the college in 1935 and served as the Administrative
ﾟilding for many years. It was torn down in the 1960s. Mount Union
ﾟllege Collection

PUBLIC MEETING!

New College Building!

ON NEXT MONDAY EVENING,

The 1st of December,

A Public Meeting will be held at MT. UNION to exhibit the PLANS & DRAWINGS of the new COLLEGE BUILDING, and to receive suggestions in regard to its SIZE AND PROPORTIONS, and whether the Committee shall construct it TWO Stories High, or whether it should be THREE Stories High, embracing a LARGE PUBLIC HALL that will seat 1400 people. The size on the ground is to be 64 feet wide by 112 feet long. Plans of location will also be exhibited The architect, COL. S. C. PORTER, of Cleveland, will be present, to

EXHIBIT BY LARGE DIAGRAMS & ORAL EXPLANATIONS

THE

Plans, Sections and Paintings

Of the new College Edifice, and also submit bill of Materials, &c.

It is important that EVERY ONE who has subscribed to the amount of $25, and indeed every other person within twenty-five miles who CARES whether the College enterprise goes on successfully and satisfactorily, **BE PRESENT** on next Monday evening. Also, persons should be present who have a proposal to submit for furnishing ANY KIND OF MATERIAL OR LABOR needed in its erection, as it is intended to close all contracts for the building in a few days, and to inaugurate measures to place Mt. Union College on a basis, inviting to enterprising and business persons to purchase homes and move into the neighborhood, and cheering to all the friends of progress and of the education of both sexes equally.

By Order of the Building Committee.

MT. UNION, Nov. 25, 1861.

This 1861 broadside announces the planned construction of a new Public Hall, now known as Chapman Hall, on the campus of Mount Union College. Mount Union College Collection

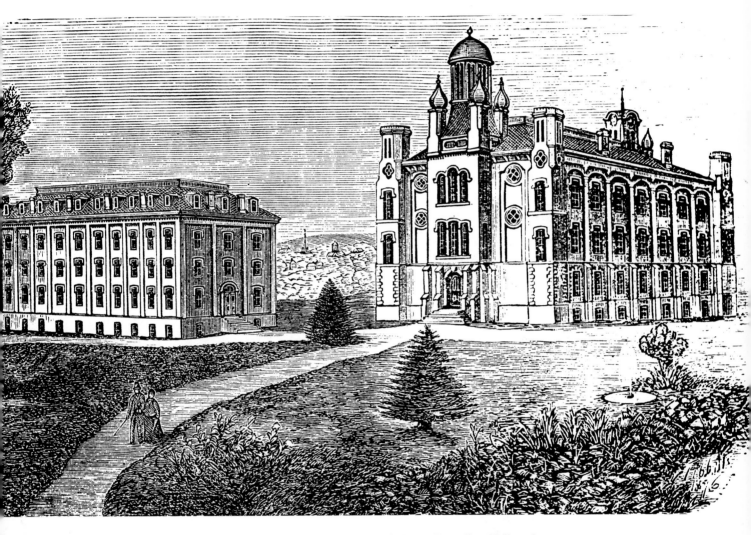

This drawing shows the Mount Union College Boarding Hall and the Main College Building, now called Chapman Hall, in 1867. The Boarding Hall is now known as Miller Hall, for Lewis Miller of Greentown who was president of the college Board of Trustees and a founder of the Chautauqua Institute in New York State. Mount Union College

The Plum Street Elementary School students pose around 1890.
The name was changed to McKinley until the Mckinley High
School was built, then it became known as Wells Elementary.
Karl Harsh Collection

TIED TO THE WORLD

1880-1900

Taking a broad view of the years between the Civil War and World War I, Stark County growth patterns took a new direction. As in many other parts of the country, these were the years when heavy industry was established—the great steel age. By its very nature the movement led many local businesses and industries into the international scene.

Companies like Morgan Engineering (Alliance), Berger Manufacturing, and Timken Rolling Bearing Company located in Stark County because of its proximity to both sources of raw materials and markets for items such as steel, like Detroit. The already established rail system in Stark County was also another attraction. Hoover, (which had changed to making suction sweepers), Diebold, McCaskey Register, Belden Brick, and Dueber Hampden Watch Factory are only a few of the many corporations founded in or moved to Stark County during the industrial period.

This rise in heavy industry was paralleled by an increase in other kinds of manufacturing and business. Many new banks and retail stores began between the late 1860s and 1920. Changes in the economic base gave the social makeup a boost during the great steel age. As an example, agriculture continued in importance, with the peak years for Stark County occurring during the 1880s. Then the number of farmers diminished; poorer ones with less acreage sold their land to wealthier neighbors and moved either to the cities and factory jobs or out west, where land was cheaper and more abundant.

This photo depicts Coxey's Army on the way to Washington to protest the lack of jobs during the depression which started in 1893 under President Grover Cleveland's administration (Democrat). With the election of William McKinley on November 3, 1896, jobs became more plentiful. Jacob Coxey, a Massillonian, can be seen riding in the carriage. *Repository* **Files Collection**

Research tells us that the industrial age and the Victorian period went hand in hand—therefore many grand Victorian homes were built at that time throughout Stark County by families who owned the various industrial plants. With the rural population dropping, the urbanization of the county began and the overall population rose significantly to 94,747 by 1900, which naturally created more schools and churches.

During the late 1800s, immigration began to impact the county. African-Americans had come here as early as 1817 and at

Around 1890 two well-dressed attendants pose behind the soda
fountain at Oppenheimer Drug Company which was located at
89 East Tuscarawas at Cherry Street, on the northwest corner.
Alice Jenkins Collection

Bender's Taproom is shown in 1902 after they moved to the Belmont Building, located on Court Avenue between Tuscarawas and Second Street Southwest. In later years the bar was moved to the other side of the room. Karl Harsh Collection

the same time many immigrants from northwestern parts of Europe came to farm. With the beginning of the twentieth century, immigration increased. The typical immigrant was more likely to be a single male from southeastern Europe, hoping to make enough money in the factories to send home to support his family. The Jewish and Greek communities were developed in the later part of the 1800s and early 1900s. For example, when Dueber Hampden Watch Works moved its plant from Springfield, Massachusetts, to Canton in 1886, it also brought four hundred employees and their families. Many of these were from Switzerland and Germany.

The increase in industrialization and urbanization of Stark County resulted in an increase in human services, notably those run by charitable organizations. These services joined education and religion as an important part of county life. Interest in providing human services

In May 1899, this drawing was featured in *The Repository* announcing a new building designed by architect Guy Tilden. Today we know it as the home of Bender's Restaurant. Craig Bara Collection

A group of men pose with their rifles near the Stark County Fairgrounds at Canton's Nimishillen Park in 1892. Standing are: Miller, Greminger, James Barry, George L. Lawrence, Thomas Bolton, Dr. William Warren, Edward Goldberg, Oberlin, H. Smith, Dr. Becher, and Dr. Ed Brant. Sitting are: Grantley Robbins, J. J. Oldfield, Henry Wise, P. P. Bush, Frank Schiltz, Cyrus Bostick, John L. Lynch, Louis J. Miday, Paul Gschwend, and Fred Lied. Stark County Historical Society Collection

Peter Daniel Keplinger (standing) was owner and proprietor of the Keplinger House, one of the early small hotels of the city. The bowler men and the dog (corner of porch) are unidentified. It was located at the southeast corner of Main Street and Linden Avenue and was later known as the Lexington Hotel. Alliance Historical Society Collection

Henry Timken (1831–1910) was the founder of the Timken Roller Bearing Axle Company in 1899. Timken Company Files

The New Berlin Cornet band was organized in 1873. this picture was taken September 23, 1897. The Heritage Society of North Canton

The George Deuble Jewelry Store was located for many years in this building at 130 South Market Street in Canton (between Second and Tuscarawas on the east side). The store was founded in 1855. *1896 Atlas*

The Canton Post Office was built in 1890 and razed in 1930. The bricks were used to build the Fawcett home at Twenty-second Street Northwest. A newer building was erected for the Post Office which is now the Frank T. Bow Building at Cleveland to Dewalt and Second Street to Third Street South. *Repository* Files Collection

New Berlin School children pose around 1884. Heritage Information Center Collection

can probably be explained by the large number of urban poor, many of whom could not read or write.

Organizations began as early as 1866 with the founding of the Young Men's Christian Association, which was reorganized in 1886. It was followed by Citadels of the Salvation Army in Canton in 1884, Massillon in 1885, and Alliance in 1886 and the Association of Charities in 1887. The first hospital was Aultman, which opened in 1892.

This era was not only known as the Steel Age or period of industrial revolution, but was also known as the McKinley Era. Although it spills over into the next century, it started in 1867 when Major William McKinley, straight from Albany Law School of New York, came to Canton. He was born in Niles, Ohio, and distinguished himself in the Civil War. Most probably because his sister, Anna, lived and taught school in Canton, McKinley selected the town for his legal practice.

At that time Canton's population was about seventy-five hundred. His move toward success started immediately. Within a year, he was elected president of the YMCA and was a favorite Republican speaker for miles around. In succession, he became county prosecutor (1868), then married Ida Saxton (1871), and ran successfully for Congress. After serving there from 1876 to

The first New Berlin (North Canton) baseball team poses in 1898. In the front row, from left to right, are: H. W. Hoover, Clarence Schiltz, Fred Kreighbaum, Ellis Schiltz, and John Evans, Jr. In the back row are: C. Ross, Wise, Wally Schick, Emery Saylor, and W. J. Evans. The Heritage Society of North Canton

Women workers at the Hoover Leather Factory in New Berlin (North Canton), circa 1885. In the front row, from left to right, are: Alice Hershey Coggler, Ann Wise Winnell, Gertrude Meckle, Effie Beasecker Givler, unknown, Maude Hershey White, and Emma Warburton Gottschall. In the middle row are: Clara Willaman, Grace Snyder, Pearl Coleman, Emma Willaman Warburton, Myme Evans Schick, Selma Hibschman, Irene Hower, and unknown. In the back row are: Nell Coleman, Clara Saylor, Mary Humbach Troxell, Clara Willaman, Maggie Evans, Nell Willaman Kreighbaum, and Emma Holl Wernet. The Heritage Society of North Canton

Interior of the Grand Opera House located in the 100 block of Third Street Southeast, circa 1895. Classic Car Museum Collection

From 1820 to 1860 a small community and school was known as *Slabtown* because of the sawmill in operation there. From 1860 to 1900 it was called *Clayshaft* because of the clay mine nearby. In 1900 the Standard Bolt and Manufacturing Company opened and the school and village adopted the name *Bolton*. The community is now part of Alliance. Alliance Historical Society Collection

Right: William McKinley giving an address on Women's Day 1896 at the Carnahan Home on West Tuscarawas Street. *Repository* Files Collection

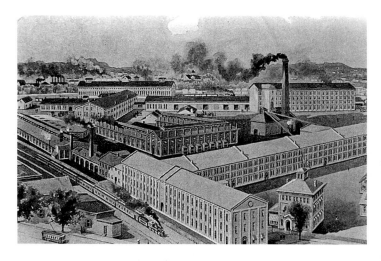

The Wrought Iron Bridge Company was founded in 1869.
1896 Atlas

Right: Samuel Luntz founded the Canton Iron and Metal
Company in 1898, which became the Luntz Corporation
early in the twentieth century. Luntz Family Collection

The Weber Dental Manufacturing Company on Mahoning Road
was in the building originally constructed to house Frank E.
Case's Harvard Company, which manufactured dental and
surgical chairs. The Romanesque Revival style building was
designed by Guy Tilden in 1896. *Repository* Files Collection

The McKinley Home in the late 1890s.
Repository Files Collection

Elmore Willis, a Canton policeman, posed
for his portrait around 1899. Mary Willis
Collection

Mr. and Mrs. Fred E. Kessel, posing in his handmade car in 1902. Mr. Kessel built the car by hand from 1899 to 1902. It went about ten feet on its first run. By clamping weights between the spokes on the flywheel, it attained a speed of ten to fifteen miles per hour. This is believed to be the first handmade car in Massillon. Betty Kress Collection

v. Eli Washington John Lindesmith, a Catholic Priest, ped to organize many of the Catholic churches in Stark unty. He also served as a U.S. Army chaplain at Fort ogh in Montana. While there, Father Lindesmith became authority and collector of Indian art. In his later years he ped organize the "Total Abstinence Society" and lectured en on the subject. He lived to be ninety-five years old. ther Kolp Collection

ft: President McKinley at his desk at the executive office the White House. *Repository* Files Collection

Miss Anna Bell and her sister Mrs. Naomi Granger were genial owners of Alliance's famous Temple of Economy, a variety china and novelty shop. It was located at the north east corner of Main Street and Mechanic Avenue. Here we see in this 1899 photo the original frame building sitting in the middle of Mechanic Street while the W. K. Fogg Building is being built. They would occupy the new building for a number of years. Many would remember this building in later years as the Owl Grill. Alliance Historical Society Collection

The J. W. McClymond's home "Five Oaks" on Fourth Street
was built in 1894 and later became the Massillon Woman's Club
(1924) when daughters Ruth and Edna, shown in the photo,
donated the home to the women of Massillon. Massillon Museum
Collection

Left: Joseph Davenport founded the Massillon Bridge Company.
He invented the cantilever bridge and the cow catcher mounted
on the front of railroad engines to push cattle off the tracks.
Massillon Museum Collection

Right: Elizabeth Robinson Bowman, wife of George Bowman.
Her grandparents were "freed" and purchased land here in 1810.
They were the first African Americans in the Massillon area.
Marva Dotson Collection

The Warwick Building was built in 1888 and razed in 1975. The Massillon Post Office was the farthest "shop" on right (north end). Massillon Museum Collection

Canal Fulton on the west side of South Canal Street looking north, circa 1890. Canal Fulton Heritage Society Collection

Top: Building the reservoir dam and spillway in 1886, now Sippo Park in Massillon. Massillon Museum Collection

The Canton Business College, where penmanship was made a specialty, was located on the southwest corner of Tuscarawas and Market Streets where Bank One is today. *Canton of Today — 1890*

The Great Western Opera House at Cherry and Canal Streets in Canal Fulton is shown circa 1898. Canal Fulton Heritage Society Collection

1890, he became governor of Ohio and served two terms. In 1896 he was elected president of the United States and re-elected in 1900.

William McKinley brought Canton and Stark County to national and worldwide attention by his "Front Porch Presidential Campaign," which he conducted from his home at Eighth Street and Market Avenue North in Canton. Instead of going about the country, a variety of delegations came here to see and interview him, and a special election issue of *The Repository* was printed and distributed nationally. Of course, the international press also came here to cover the campaign.

The Canton Bicycle Club was organized in 1883 and incorporated in 1887. When this photo was taken in 1890, the officers were C. W. Keplinger (president), Guy Tilden (vice president), and Will G. Saxton (secretary/treasurer). *Canton of Today—1890.*

The Hampden Watch Works were constructed in 1888 on Deuber Avenue (Canton). Canton Museum of Art Collection

Morgan Gymnasium in Alliance was dedicated in 1891. It was named for Industrialist Thomas R. Morgan who financially supported the construction of this building. Mount Union College's first intercollegiate basketball game was held here in 1896. Alliance Historical Society, Mount Union College

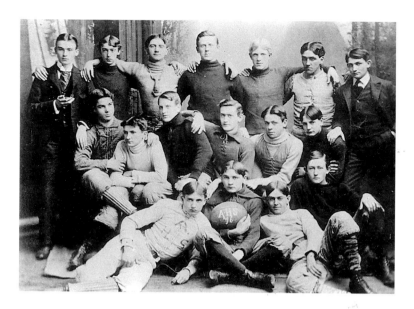

Alliance High School's second football team in 1896. In the top row, from left to right, are: Orville Witter, Roy Forbes, Ralph Shaffer, Dick Hoiles, Russell Armstrong, Alexander Robinson, and Brian Ensign. In the second row are: Charles Heer, Howard Burtz, Erb Lewis, Frank Tombaugh, George Vander Par, and Bob Shaffer. In the third row are: Fred Southworth, Dutch Myers, Rush Clark, and Lawrence Hutchinson. Alliance Historical Society Collection

Constructed in 1894 in Alliance, this Queen Anne House was the home and office of Dr. Charles E. Rice, a local dentist. He was also a prominent figure at Mount Union College serving as treasurer and secretary for many years. Known for his collection of furniture and historical documents, he had in his possession the fireplace from Lincoln's home in Illinois and a Gilbert Stuart painting of George Washington. After his death in 1939 his estate was sold at a three-day auction at Mount Union College. Craig Bara Collection

This view of a snowy day shows the south side of the 400 block of Main Street. Some of the businesses were Keplinger Hotel, C. Y. Kay Hardware Store, and Wright and Pennock Hardware on the square. Alliance Historical Society Collection

This 1897 photo shows the newly completed Mount Union Methodist Episcopal Church on South Union Avenue in Alliance. Known as the "College Church," the cornerstone was laid after commencement on July 13, 1893, by then college Trustee and Ohio Governor William McKinley and church Bishop Edwin Joyce. Craig Bara Collection

own under construction in the 1900s, this home as the iontown Hospital during the 1920s. May Parsons llection

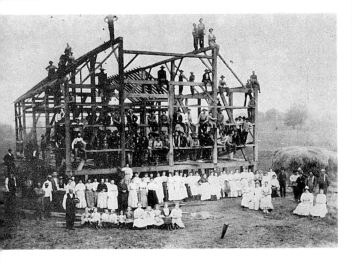

barn raising in Canal Fulton. Canal Fulton Heritage ciety Collection

John P. Barker, shown here around 1885, is believed to have been Canton's first lamplighter. Warren Okey Collection

A family and their cows along the Ohio Canal. Navarre
Bethlehem Historical Society

The Hall Building at Massillon State Hospital is shown during its construction in 1898. It was demolished in 1986. This building was considered one of the best examples in Ohio of the cottage plan design for a state institution. During McKinley's years as governor he authorized the construction of the institute, then known as the Eastern Ohio Asylum for the insane. Stark County Historical Society Collection, *The Repository*

Plain Township Revival Tent, circa 1890. Richard Uhrich Collection

Left: The Warrick and Justus Flour Mill in Massillon. Circa 1880. Massillon Museum Collection

Right: Abel Fletcher, the inventor of paper negatives, shot this photograph of downtown Massillon around 1845. Massillon Museum Collection

Flood in downtown Massillon. Massillon Museum Collection

The McGinty Tile Plant employees pose for a company portrait at the plant on Maplegrove Road, around 1900. Louisville Public Library Collection

Ready to deliver by horse and buggy, the mail carriers stand proudly in front of the Post Office in the 200 block of East Main Street in this 1890s photo. From left to right are: M. L. Justus, Harvey Criswell, Harry Warstler, Frank Sluss, and Harvey Royer. Louisville Public Library Collection

This 1893 photo shows the Kagey Brothers Cash Grocers on East Main Street in Louisville. Standing in front are Mr. William H. Kagey (proprietor) Ms. Saejot (hired for her ability to speak French) and Mr. John B. Kagey (proprietor). Louisville Public Library Collection

The employees of the corn rolling mills in Massillon posed around 1880. Massillon Museum Collection

Louisville's returning veterans of the Spanish-American War. From left to right in the front row are: August Balizet, Paul Chevraux, Lincoln Slusser, and Frank Kutz. In the back are: John George, John Newhouse, George Thurin, and unknown. Louisville Public Library Collection

Shown here are the employees at a glass factory in Massillon. Glass making was a major industry from 1880 to 1920. Massillon Museum Collection

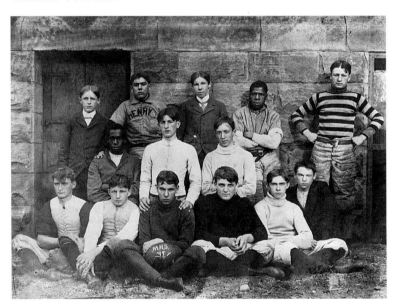

Massillon Tigers Football Team. Massillon Museum Collection

The dance hall pavilion at Lake Chautauqua (located east of Alliance) was the area's number one summer entertainment spot at the turn of the century. Also visible in the 1890s photo is the Power House for the Stark Electric Street Car Company which used the lake to cool down its generators. Alliance Historical Society Collection

Dan Sheldon and friends at "Live and Let Live" Saloon on Market Street (west of river). Canal Fulton Heritage Society Collection

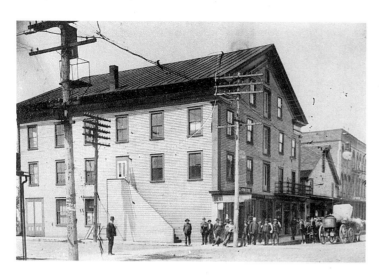

Left: The Great Western Opera House was located at Cherry and Canal Streets. Canal Fulton Heritage Society Collection

Right: This Methodist Church was on Cherry Street. Canal Fulton Heritage Society Collection

The Barnes Grocery Store was located in the Stroup Building on the northwest corner of Mount Union Square about 1906. This building has housed numerous businesses including a hardware store, Turner's Drug Store, Isaly's Dairy, and Mount Union Square Pharmacy. Mount Union Square Pharmacy

The Oberlin House in Canal Fulton is shown in 1897. Pictured are Sarah and Christian Oberlin. It is now the home of the Canal Fulton Heritage Society. Canal Fulton Heritage Society Collection

The Canal Fulton School, shown here in 1886, was situated between Market and Cherry Streets at Locust. Canal Fulton Heritage Society Collection

This is the 1897 Street Fair at Canal Fulton. Canal Fulton
Heritage Society Collection

Main Street in Alliance looking west from the viaduct, circa 1899.
Alliance Historical Society Collection

Canton was a flurry of activity during McKinley's 1896 Front Porch Campaign. This photo was taken from the southwest corner of the square looking down East Tuscarawas Street. It shows the arrival of one of the many delegations that traveled to hear the candidate speak. *Repository* Files Collection

This threshing rig and its crew are ready for the fall harvest, circa 1895. Karl Harsh Collection

Exterior of the Evangelical United Church at 600 East Gorgas Street in Louisville, circa 1890.

The members of the Canton Thayer Military Band, Fifth Ohio Regiment, gather at Meyers Lake about 1898. Karl Harsh Collection

Harrisburg School students pose in 1897. The teacher has been
identified as Charles F. Chenot. Louisville Public Library
Collection

This picture was taken around 1915 at the Wheeling and Lake Erie Railroad yard. Those pictured from left to right are: W. M. Bainter, J. H. Hoobler, H. C. Rowe, and George Durham. CC&S Railroad Club Collection

McKINLEY, BRICKS, AND THE CARNATION

1900-1920

William McKinley was shot by an assassin in Buffalo, New York, on September 6, 1901, dying eight days later. His tomb and monument were erected and dedicated in Canton in 1907. The memorial to the fallen president was made possible, in part, by the donations of pennies by schoolchildren. Mrs. McKinley survived her husband for almost seven years. They are both buried at the monument along with their two small children.

During the funeral and the dedication of the monument, Theodore Roosevelt, who succeeded McKinley as president, came to Canton and spoke numerous times. Many Americans came here to honor his memory when the monument was dedicated. And since then, tens of thousands have visited his final resting place. In his honor many landmarks and institutions in the area were named "McKinley" (Avenue, Park, Law School, Hotel, and various organizations).

In 1914 the sounds of the War in Europe could be heard in America. The entry of the United States in 1917 brought the men and industry of Stark County into a global affair that we know as World War I. By this time, many of the male youths who made up the work force in industry were strong, young men who also worked on the family farm. When the volunteers were assigned to training camps, it was often somewhere in Ohio.

War gardens were planted to raise crops for the various neighborhoods, Liberty Bond rallies were held, and Thrift Clubs were organized. In one community, a poetry contest was held

Clara Wolf Nichols won first prize in a *Repository* contest for cooking and household hints, around 1919. Carol James Collection

among the schoolchildren and prizes of Thrift Stamps were given to the winners who penned the best verse in support of the boys in uniform. One of the winning entries was:

Buy a "Thrift Stamp" if you can

It will help good Uncle Sam,

To win the war across the sea;

To back the Sammie that fights for me.

At the beginning of the new century, the personal transportation of Stark Countians was improved with the opening of the streetcar line that came south from Cleveland through Akron, on to New Berlin, then to Canton and places south, and back. The Northern Ohio Light and Traction Company provided service on electric streetcars. Between the towns, the rails followed the highways at the side of the road, but when they continued through the towns, the lines were laid down the middle of the street.

The streetcars were often not on schedule and they

This photograph was taken September 19, 1901, at a site in northeast Canton temporarily set up for the military contingent that traveled here to participate in President William McKinley's funeral. Karl Harsh Collection

The Uniontown Fourth of July was always celebrated on the Uniontown Square, followed by a picnic at   the St. John's Lutheran Church. May Parsons Collection

Above and Left: Designed by Guy Tilden, Case Mansion was originally the home of Frank E. Case. In the 1940s it became the home of the Canton Museum of Art. Stark County Historical Society

experienced many breakdowns. They ran almost thirty years and during that time most of the county and village roads were improved with brick surfaces. But by 1930, with more and more automobiles and other difficulties, the streetcar lines closed.

Human services became more significant after World War I. The American Legion, a national organization, was established to protect the families of servicemen and to administer to the veterans in hospitals and their families. Goodwill Industries was founded in 1920, Canton Welfare Federation and Canton Community Chest (forerunner of United Way) were organized in 1922. Already established were Alliance City Hospital in 1900, Massillon Community Hospital and the county Visiting Nurse Society in 1905, and in 1908 Mercy Hospital opened its doors.

The first brickyard in Stark County was established by George Williams in 1820 at Canton, operating until the 1850s. The tradition of brick and tile making has affected many communities in Stark County. Some began in the early days in various communities, then moved on leaving the village without an important industry. Others experienced having their towns grow because of a brick or tile company. From 1820 until the 1880s a number of companies in Canton, Massillon, and Alliance were very successful. Most of them were in business for ten or more years.

"M. J. Shea—Theoretical and Practical Horse Shoer" was located at the corner of Walnut and Second Street Northeast in Canton. Shea went into business in the early 1890s and is shown here around 1905. Alice Jenkins Collection

Stark County has always been rich with what it takes to make brick and tile products. As technology improved the more successful companies bought out the small owners. Bricks were made for street paving, building construction, and ornamental uses. Tiles were mostly used to build sewer systems, flower pots, and roofing. Bricks were made by hand and machines.

The Metropolitan Brick Company, which became the world's largest paving-brick manufacturer, began in 1908 when it purchased Cleveland Brick Company, which was located in Canton and had been founded in 1888. The well-known Belden Brick Company began in 1895. Robinson Clay Products in Malvern operated from 1920 to 1957. At Waynesburg, the Whiteacre Greer Fireproofing Company incorporated in 1916 and continued until 1975.

In 1905 the scarlet carnation was selected as the state flower by the Ohio General Assembly. Stark County played an important role in that decision. Dr. Levi Leslie Lamborn of Alliance perfected the chosen flower. Lamborn was born and raised in Lexington Township. His hobby was the cultivation of flowers. He was also editor of the first newspaper in Alliance— *Alliance Ledger*. He was a prime mover in real estate, industry, banking, and the railroad. Dr. Lamborn had a friendly relationship with William McKinley. He always provided McKinley with a red carnation for his lapel. When McKinley was shot in Buffalo, he had just given his red carnation to a little girl. Leroy Leslie Lamborn inherited his father's love for flowers and started the family business. Lamborn Floral Company was incorporated in 1905.

Uniontown graduation class of 1907. May Parsons Collection

The Timken Mansion, built in 1915, later became Timken Mercy Medical Center. *Repository* Files Collection

The public School Arch on West Tuscarawas Street, Canton, in memory of President William McKinley who died from an assassin's bullet on September 14, 1901. *Repository* Files Collection

Navarre milkman Fred Dugnes with his Dages and Son dairy
wagon and horse dressed in fly-shooer attire. Navarre
Bethlehem Historical Society

The *Louisville Herald* was founded in 1887 by L. P. Bissell. John Prenot, the man in white shirt sleeves, purchased and edited the paper in the early 1900s. The young boy on right is Louis Clapper who followed Prenot as owner and editor. Louisville Public Library Collection

The McKinley Monument was under construction from 1905 to 1907. Karl Harsh Collection

Henry Ford, third from the right, visited Canton March 28, 1907,
when U.S. Steel began to experiment with Alloy Steel.
Repository Files Collection

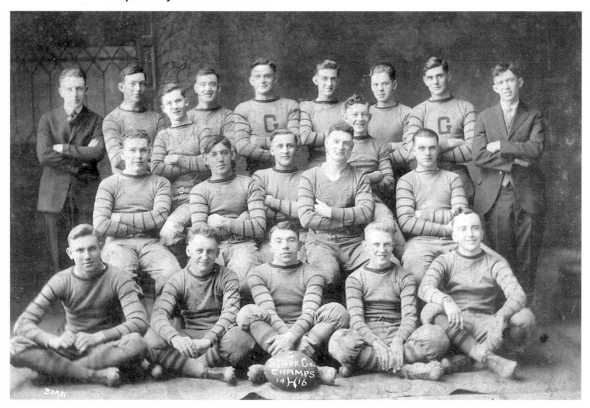

The Goat Hill Football Team pose shortly after becoming the
Stark County Champs in 1916. Alliance Historical Society
Collection

Billy Sunday was one of the most successful evangelists of the early 1900s. In the summer of 1911 preparations began for his arrival in Canton for a six-week campaign beginning December 31, 1911. Twenty-one of the twenty-six protestant churches agreed to close their churches for regular Sunday services and unite in worship at a tabernacle especially built for the occasion. A crew of 150 volunteers, ministers, and some employed carpenters erected the structure in three and a half days. It was located on the rear of the Harter property, where Memorial Auditorium now stands, on land donated by Elizabeth Harter. The building seated 8,000 and had stage capacity for a choir of 600. Despite record cold temperatures (including 24 degrees below zero on January 12th) the tabernacle had capacity audiences and thousands were turned away. People came in their sleighs from miles around and by streetcars, interurbans, and automobiles. During the six-week campaign Sunday's objective was to receive converts and to stir up church people to more active Christian lives. Five thousand people went down to the railroad station Monday, February 12, 1912, to see Billy Sunday and his party off after a successful campaign. Craig Bara Collection

A group of lovely ladies proudly show off their Sunday best about 1900. Louisville Public Library Collection

The Diebold Safe and Lock Company moved from Cincinnati to Canton and began manufacturing in 1872. Shown here are workers in 1914. Karl Harsh Collection

North High School Orchestra, 1916

The Lehman High School Basketball Team in 1924. In the back row from left to right are: Coach Bill Snyder, Weient Holmes, Jack Bahl, and Howard Greenwalt. In the front row are: Paul Cronenewit, Joe Hilton, Glen Beack, White Gale, and Robert Ewing. Lehman School Historical Collection

The Frank A. Hoiles residence was built on the corner of Union Avenue and East Milton Street. Hoiles was owner of the *Alliance Review* and president and general manager of the Alliance Brick Company. He was killed in an automobile accident on December 29, 1936. Alliance Historical Society Collection

The Central Union Telephone Company was Canton's first phone company. Canton Classic Car Museum Collection

Employees pose outside the Timken Roller Bearing Axle
Company in 1902. The Timken Company

George Bowman of Massillon operated the City
Smoke House. Farmers brought their meat to
be smoked for ten cents a piece. Marva Dotson
Collection

Left: William Rufus Day was born in Ravenna in 1849. He served in the McKinley Administration as secretary of state and chairman of the commission to negotiate the treaty of peace at the close of the Spanish-American War. After McKinley's death, Day was named to the U.S. Supreme Court as an associate justice. After retiring from that position in 1922, he was appointed by President Harding to the Mixed Claims Commission to determine the claims against Germany. He died on July 9, 1923. *Repository* Files Collection

Right: Educator Mary Ellen Bowman was born in 1858 at Massillon. She taught throughout the Great Lakes area in both public schools and colleges. Her grandparents, Issac and Rachel Robinson, purchased land in Stark County in 1810. Marva Dotson Collection

Members of the Second Baptist Church on North Union and Selby Streets in 1919. Seated from left to right are: Mrs. McDuffy, Leily Baker, Annie Jackson, Ruby Northington, and Mabel Smally. Standing are: Ruth Rhine, Robert (Unkown), Annabelle Kennedy, Horace Adams, Gertrude Head, Oscar Rhine, and D. D. Dantly. Alliance Historical Society Collection

Gertrude Griffiths, daughter of Fred J. Griffiths, lights furnaces at Central Steel Company around 1915. Massillon Museum Collection

The Canton Home Furnishing Company operated from 1899 to
1921. The truck was a two-cylinder, air cooled, chain driven
vehicle with solid rubber tires. Bruce Dunlap Collection

The Canton City Auditorium was constructed in 1904. Occupying
a full city block bounded by Fourth and Fifth Streets, Cleveland
Avenue, and Court Street. It was razed in 1956. Stark County
Regional Planning Files

The southwest corner of Public Square and Main Street was a favorite gathering spot for children in the early 1900s. Martins Confectionery was known for their homemade candy and ice cream. They also dealt in fruits and vegetables. Many buildings in this block were torn down in 1924 to make way for Alliance's new skyscraper —The City Savings and Trust Building. Alliance Historical Society Collection

The old Beckett Candy Company in Wilmot is shown about 1955. *Repository* Files Collection

Right: Mary Johnson of Massillon had been a cook for Abraham Lincoln. During World War I she joined a Red Cross nursing unit. One of her three sons, George Herman Johnson, was a well-known poet and playwright. Marva Dotson Collection

The students of Mount Union College in Alliance gleefully prepare for their march to the train station to greet the new president of the college, William Henry McMaster, about 1909. Craig Bara Collection

The Knights of Pythias Building was constructed around 1900.

Keim's Bank and Hardware on Main Street, circa 1905. Louisville
Public Library Collection

A funeral procession in front of A. H. Wilson Automobiles garage on Fifth Street Northeast, circa 1904. Note the Arnold Funeral Home Hearse. *Repository* Files Collection

Nees Rexall Pharmacy at 128 East Main Street in the early 1900s. Louisville Public Library Collection

The Beechwood E.U.B. Church was photographed about 1915.
Craig Bara Collection

This early 1900s photo shows the sales force of Geiger the Clothier, a popular men's store in downtown for many years. Pictured from left to right are: Max Geiger, Harry Roderick, and Guy Shaffer. Alliance Historical Society Collection

This is the original selling staff of the Stern and Mann Company, photographed near the turn of the century. From left to right are: Clara Lape, Julia Quinn (McCarthy), Lena Dysle, Jet Whiteleather, Winnie Newton, Mamie Wagner Miller, and Lottie Prendeville. Besides waiting on customers, each girl had her morning chores which had to be done before the store's day began. The clerks swept, dusted cases and fixtures, and arranged the stock. Lottie Prendeville was assigned the chore of filling the coal oil lamps, cleaning the chimneys, and trimming the wicks. *Repository* Files Collection

This is the interior of Stern and Mann's second store which was located on the west side of Market Avenue North and Second Street. *Repository* Files Collection

William H. Martin rides twenty-five feet above the ground in his Martin Monoplane glider in 1909, with a Ford providing power. *Repository* Files Collection

Paul Wines, aerial acrobat, poses on a grounded plane. *Repository* Files Collection

This picture was taken in front of the Post Office on Uniontown Square's southwest corner, circa 1905. May Parsons Collection

Glamorgan Castle was the residence of Col. William H. Morgan
of Morgan Engineering Company. Designed by Cleveland
architects Searles and Hirsch, it was built between 1903 and
1907. Morgan had his home copied after various baronial castles
of the Middle Ages with the most scientific and practical aids of
modern life and living. The exterior is made up entirely of
Vermont marble. Alliance Historical Society Collection

This home was built in 1908 by Walter Webb, a prominent
banker of Alliance. The Alliance Woman's Club has made its
home in this palatial structure on South Union Avenue since its
organization in 1923. Alliance Historical Society Collection

The Fairmount Grange was organized January 14, 1897, with twenty charter members. Meetings were originally held in the members' homes until this hall was constructed in 1911. It was built on land donated by Richard Washington. The Grange closed in the 1980s. Alliance Historical Society Collection

Canton's Wells School children pose for a class portrait around 1910. Karl Harsh Collection

Paving the streets in Uniontown, circa 1915. May Parsons
Collection

The Village of Justus was named in honor of Fred W. Justus
who was Massillon's postmaster for many years. The first plat
was recorded June 8, 1874, with only nine lots, all lying west of
the railroad. In this photo we see the train rolling into the
railroad station around 1900. Stark County Historical Society

The Pennsylvania Railroad Bridge in Maximo has the typical decoration—a row of barefoot boys. Craig Bara Collection

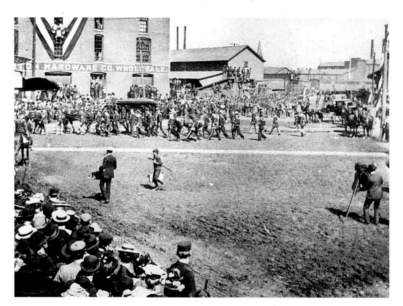

Shown here is the September 1901 funeral procession escorting McKinley's hearse from the Pennsylvania station. They are heading to downtown Canton on Fifth Street Southeast (the camera is located at corner of Sixth Street and Savannah Avenue Southeast). President Theodore Roosevelt was riding behind McKinley in a carriage owned by Col. William Morgan of Alliance. Note that the cameramen at left has a movie camera. This photo was discovered in an attic and given to the Canton Hardware Company since their building is so prominent in the picture. Tom Kendle Collection

New Berlin (North Canton) children pose around 1910 in front of
the school built in 1890. Stark County Historical Society

The north front of Russell and Company, manufacturers of engines, sawmills, and threshing machines was photographed May 5, 1908. Massillon Museum Collection

In 1902 one of Minerva's most important industries began with the founding of the Owen China Company, the first pottery in town. The company employed 300 to 400 people producing semi-porcelain dinnerware. The pottery industry suffered severely in the Depression of the 1930s and Owen became a casualty. It was bought in 1934 by the Cronin family who modernized the plant. They were purchased by the U.S. Ceramic Tile Company in 1956 which ceased producing porcelainware and began the production of glazed tile.
Stark County Historical Society

A Memorial Day Parade, circa 1915. No matter how bad the weather or the road, the paraders trudged on to decorate the graves. The Heritage Society of North Canton

The Carnegie Free Library was built in Alliance in 1903. As in many other small towns, the money to build the library was given through the generosity of Andrew Carnegie. The money was given to communities that put forward great effort and showed a true commitment to education. Alliance Historical Society Collection

After operating for fourteen years it became apparent to the trustees of the hospital association that more finances and a modern building would be required for Alliance City Hospital. A bond issue was passed amounting to $50,000. A new building (pictured) was designed by Architect Willard Hirsh of Cleveland. Construction was completed and the new building was opened to the public January 1, 1917. The annex on the back was added in the 1920s. Alliance Historical Society Collection

The original Hoover factory building near the North Canton Square on East Maple Street, circa 1910. Heritage Information Center Collection

**Charles Gaume was the Louisville lamplighter in 1903. Louisville
Public Library Collection**

Santa Claus visits downtown Louisville and takes the schoolchildren for a truck ride through the streets. Children provided their own music with horns and noise makers. Festivities ended with the singing of Christmas carols and Santa throwing candy to the children. This was an annual event sponsored by businessmen during World War I. Louisville Public Library Collection

Left: The *Canton Daily News* was known for its progressivism and promotion of civic reform. Publisher Don R. Mellet was ambushed and murdered in July 1926 for exposing the underworld which was strongly established in Canton. This structure was built in 1912. Stark County Regional Planning Files

This photo shows the third building occupied by Stern and Mann. They moved into this structure in 1912 in Canton when they incorporated, giving them 1,600 square feet of floor space. Located on Market Avenue North they remained there until the new building at Tuscarawas and Cleveland Avenue was completed in 1925, giving them 40,000 square feet of sales floor. This building became part of McCrorys a few years later. *Repository* Files Collection

Right: Stern and Mann's first delivery service was by bicycle, of which the firm's founder was extremely proud. *Repository* Files Collection

Kindergarten children at Fairmount Childrens Home play games at a party, circa 1905. Craig Bara Collection

The Alliance City Hall was built between 1912 and 1915. Alliance Historical Society Collection

Left: The Navarre Band members pose in front of the fire station around 1900. Navarre Bethlehem Historical Society

Right: Farmers collect wheat in the fields of Nimishillen Township during the early 1900s. Louisville Public Library Collection

Pennsylvania Station, located on Market Avenue South in Canton, was constructed in 1916 by the Pennsylvania Railroad. The structure was a fine example of the Beaux-Arts Classical Revival style of architecture. With the growth of the interstate highway system in the 1950s, railroad passenger service was adversely affected. The station closed in the early 1970s and was demolished in 1976. Stark County Historical Society Collection

This photograph was taken in December 1907. It shows Frances E. Miday, age two, with her sister Mary, eleven months. Mary became a noted scholar and translator of numerous French books. On a Fulbright Scholarship, she took thousands of pictures throughout France during the time Charles DeGaulle was president. She died in 1994. Frances spent her life as an auditor and evangelist. Ruth E. Whitticar Collection

A severe snowstorm hit downtown Canton, February 16, 1910.
Note the streetcar tracks. Karl Harsh Collection

Kagey's Grocery Store operated at 125 East Main Street,
Louisville. The clerk is Cora Emerson, about 1920. Louisville
Public Library Collection

Early employees of the Bell Telephone Company pose around
1912. The first telephone switchboard was installed in Canton
December 12, 1880. Thomas Kendle Collection

The Players Club performed at the Empire Theater in Alliance about 1915. From left to right are: George Thurin, unknown, Martha Metzger, Mae Rebrassier, James Dwyer, Mildred Shearer, unknown, unknown, Berdette Shearer, unknown, and unknown. Louisville Public Library Collection

Woman's Suffrage parade in Louisville in 1920. Louisville Public Library Collection

Panoramic view of Uniontown, circa 1900. May Parsons Collection

Interior of Schroeder's Meat Market in Canal Fulton. Canal Fulton Heritage Society Collection

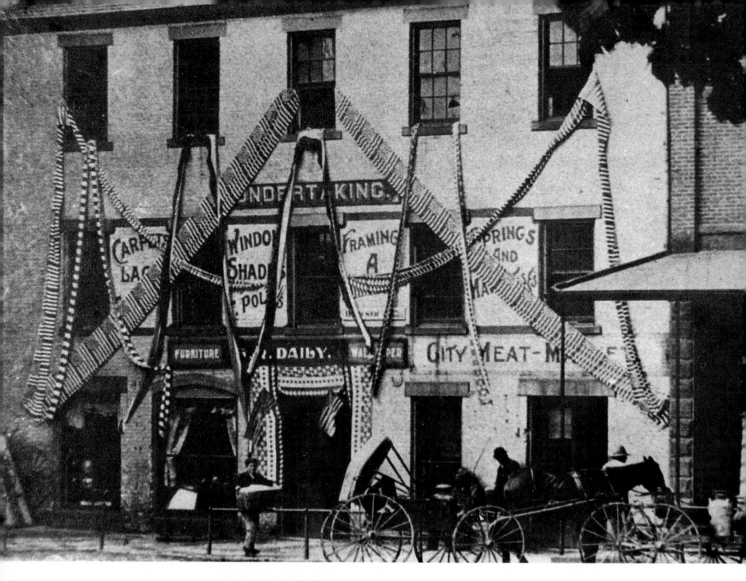

C. R. Daily Furniture and Undertaker operated on the west side of Canal Street between the Held and Oddfellows Buildings. Canal Fulton Heritage Society Collection

Right: The 1913 Flood leaves these residents undaunted at Canal Fulton. Canal Fulton Heritage Society Collection

**The 1904 flood at Canal Fulton, looking south from Cereal Mill.
Canal Fulton Heritage Society Collection**

**The Canal Fulton Imperial Band, from a 1904 family reunion at
Luna Lake. Canal Fulton Heritage Society Collection**

The train carrying President William McKinley's body was heavily draped in black. Members of the crowd seem eager just to touch the engine. Karl Harsh Collection

Men install telephone lines in Canal Fulton in 1901 on Brimstone Corners looking south on Canal Street. Canal Fulton Heritage Society Collection

Brimstone under water looking west, circa 1913. Canal Fulton Heritage Society Collection.

At *The Repository* an editor, pressman, and commercial artist work on a graphic of downtown Canton about 1905. *Repository* Files Collection

This bird's-eye view of Beach City, Ohio, was taken in 1908. Bill Haldi Collection

Bottom Right: The Ohio readies for take off July 23, 1908. Pictured from left to right are: George B. Frease, Charles Daugherty, Dr. W. D. Sigler of Salem, Leo Stevens (pilot), Louis Brush of Salem, Johnson Sherrick, and Joseph M. Blake. The two children in front are unidentified. *Repository* Files Collection

This photograph, taken at Navarre Square, depicts the largest log shipped by railroad from Navarre (1916). The driver is Ohio Snyder and the horses are Clyde and Rudy. The man to the left is unidentified. Navarre Bethlehem Historical Society Collection

The "All America" balloon fills with natural gas at ascension field at the end of Walnut Avenue Southeast in 1909. *Repository Files Collection*

Above: The Hurford Hotel opened as the Franklin House around 1858. After a fire in the 1860s it reopened as the St. Cloud Hotel. In 1890 it became the Hurford Hotel. This building was razed in 1901 to make way for the Courtland Hotel which opened in 1905. *Repository* Files Collection

In the early 1900s the largest foreign-born population in Alliance was the Hungarians. They organized their first church session in 1907 and built this house of worship in 1909 on East Cambridge Street, shown here on the occasion of its first funeral service. Their old world customs and traditions are evident. With the declining Hungarian and Transylvanian population, the church was forced to close in 1970s and was torn down soon after. Craig Bara Collection

The young men of the Louisville Drum Corps, circa 1910. In the first row from left to right are: Edward Clapper, Harry Bailet, and unknown. In the second row are: Marion Thurin, Lloyd Devaux, and unknown. In the third row are: Schloneger, Louis Clapper, Frank Clapper, unknown, unknown, unknown, Jame Dwyer, and unknown. Louisville Public Library Collection

Billings Dry Goods Store of Canal Fulton is shown about 1900.
Canal Fulton Heritage Society Collection

The Rinehart Varieties Company in Louisville was the
manufacturer of celluloid pinwheel toys. Here we see the
employees posing in front of the factory in 1909. Louisville
Public Library Collection

Union Railway Depot, Navarre, Ohio, U. S A,

The sign on Navarre's Union Railway Depot reads "Wheeling &
Lake Erie R.R. and Wabash System. Take trains here for
Pittsburgh, Wheeling, Cleveland, Zanesville, Toledo, Detroit,
Chicago, St. Louis, Kansas City, Omaha, and all points north,
south, east, and west." Navarre Bethlehem Township Collection

1910 New Berlin (now North Canton) community football team. In the first row from left to right are: John Pfouts, Clarence Snyder, Gilbert Hibshan, Lawrence Acker, Bill Volker, Joe Ebie, Roy Saylor, and Clem Willaman. In the second row are: Emen Clouser, Wallace Willaman, Ray Evans, Harry Willaman, Earl Schick, Arch Swope, Austin Schlitz, Fred Kreighbaum, and Ben Daugherty. Richard Uhrich Collection

**Fourteen Palace Theatre ushers photographed in 1928.
Donald Ingold Collection**

ALL THAT IT TAKES

1920-1940

As the steel age moved farther into the new century, the last development was culture. As leisure time increased, so did the desire to take part in cultural activities. Already in Canton was the Opera House and in the late nineteenth century, popular culture centered around participation in singing societies. The twentieth century saw a shift from participation to observation with the founding of the Canton Symphony in 1903, the Players Guild in 1932, and the Canton Museum of Art in 1934. Popular interest in these strong organizations continues as we move into the twenty-first century.

During the latter part of the teens, from 1916 to 1918, the first wing of McKinley High School was constructed followed by a second wing in 1920–1921. By this time most schools in Stark County were graded, meaning that each grade level would have its own room and teacher.

The timeline of Stark County from 1920 to 1940 is a long list of community services which began in that era, school building and curriculum expansion, along with significant media advances and the founding of many social groups. Considering that a national depression undermined the economy of the United States in the middle of this period, it is something of a miracle that the county made such grand progress.

Canton's Rev. L. L. Slaughter was the first African- American Boy Scout Leader in the United States. Urban League Files

Community Services established from 1920 to 1929 are as follows:

Canton Urban League	1920
Massillon YWCA	1921
Boy Scout Council	1921
Canton Welfare Federation	1922
North Canton Community Building–YMCA	1923
Girl Scout Council/Camp	1924
Philamatheon Society	1924
Massillon YMCA	1925
Alliance YWCA	1926
National Guard Armory	1926
Molly Stark Sanatorium	1929

School history was heightened by the following:

The first student Police Patrol in the United States was established at Canton's Worley School in 1922

St. John's Catholic School was founded in 1925

William McKinley Law School opened in 1926

Canton Fawcett Stadium was built in 1937—A Works Progress Administration (WPA) project

Timken Vocational High School was opened in 1939

Media began to play a major role as Stark County grew: the following were established during this period:

Stark County Jewish News	1920
North Canton Sun	1923
WHBC founded as church station for shut-ins	1925
WHBC Mutual Broadcasting Co.	1939
Brush-Moore buys the *Repository*	1927
Brush-Moore buys the *Canton Daily News*	1930
Canton Economist	1932

The social scene was enhanced by the founding of the following:

Canton American Legion Post 44	1920
Canton Jewish Center	1924
Palace Theatre	1926
Swiss Club	1928
Players Guild	1932
Massillon Museum	1933
Canton Museum of Art	1934
Canton Jaycees	1934
Canton Music Association	1935
Canton Park System	1936
Alliance Historical Society	1939
Stark County Historical Society	1946

During this same era the magnificent Onesto Hotel was built in 1930. That same year, the Halle Brothers Company of Cleveland selected Canton for their second store site. Such businesses as Ashland Oil, Franz-Royer Electric Company, Sugardale Foods, Buxbaum, Ohio Ferro Alloy, and Republic Steel were founded here between 1924 and 1930. As another sign of the times, automobile agencies became popular businesses.

As student bodies became caught up with the various school teams, mascots were being selected, school songs written, school colors chosen and the tradition of social events for young people began to center around extra-curricular activities at school. Language and science clubs became popular among students as did drama productions.

It would seem that as the 1930s ended, Stark County was prepared for anything. The highways that linked the various centers were improved as more and more automobiles were purchased, schools of special learning were opening for subjects not found in public schools, and the social balance of the county offset the human needs of some of its citizens. Stark County had everything it would take to enter the new decade. War was not on the agenda.

The Arcade Market locate at Arch Street and Prospect was built
in the late 1920s in Alliance. It was the largest commercial
building in Alliance for many years. Today it is the home of the
Sherwood Factory Outlet. Alliance Historical Society Collection

Christmas at the Arcade Market during the 1920s. Some of the
popular vendors during the '20s and '30s were Meadowbrooks,
Joe Migal's Fruit and Vegetable Stand, Market House Grocery,
and Warren and Zella Baker—Proprietors, and Harwicks
Vegetable and Dry Goods Stand. Alliance Historical Society
Collection

Garfield School, circa 1930. Karl Harsh Collection

Mennonite children at school located at Lake Center and King
Church Road, Uniontown, circa 1920. Anonymous Donor
Collection

This 1926 view shows the southwest corner of Main Street and Arch Street in Alliance. Some of the occupants in the block were Valis Confectionery and Cigar Store, State Theater, Cohn's Dry Goods, and Baughman's Grocery. Note the Stark Electric Streetcar tracks and the traffic light in the center of the street. Alliance Historical Society Collection

The North Canton Championship team won the class "B" state title in 1939. In the front row from left to right are: Roy Mohler, William Ashbaugh, Benjamin Swarner, Charles Murphy, Sterling Pollock, and Joseph Peters. In the back row are: Max Rohrer, Harvey Sponseller, Robert D. Ginther, Ray Swope, William Lowther, Harold "Jim" Sponseller, and Charles Bruhn. Others on the team were Robert L. Ginther, Robert VanHorn, Dale Wearstler, and Kenneth Warburton. Heritage Information Center Collection

The Original North Canton Community Building (YMCA) opened
in 1923, a gift to the community from W. H. "Boss" Hoover. Bill
Cumler Collection

Three horse-drawn wagons, two trucks, and one company car made up the Superior Dairy fleet shown in this photo taken in 1924 on Navarre Road, Southwest in Canton. Superior Dairy Collection

Top: This picture was taken at a picnic of the Canton Tin Plate Corporation, circa 1922. Karl Harsh Collection

Left: Newlyweds August Sagermann, Canton Print Shop proprietor, and his wife Nettie pose with their new 1923 Chandler "8." The maroon car is believed to have been the first one in Canton with a finish other than black. Lewis Sagermann Collection

Right: The Landing at Meyers Lake looking north, circa 1925. Karl Harsh Collection

On December 24, 1933, the First Brethren Church of Louisville presented "At the Door of the Inn." Louisville Public Library Collection

The Palace Theatre at the corner of Sixth Street and Market Avenue North (Canton) was built in 1926, shown here in 1954, and is the last vestige of the early elegant theater houses in Stark County. Marcella Emmons Collection

Above: An unknown child takes a ride in a goat cart, circa 1924. Goat and wagon owners went throughout the city neighborhoods giving children rides for a small fee. Norma Boscia Collection

Left: The Ohio Power Company building at Second Street and Cleveland Avenue South is all decked out for the holidays, circa 1939. Marcella Emmons Collection

Airplane made in Massillon, circa 1920. Massillon Museum Collection

Union Newsstand at the Pennsylvania Railroad Station October 2, 1927. Alliance Historical Society Collection

The north side of Main Street between Freedom and Seneca in Alliance was like a complete town condensed into one area in 1930 when this picture was taken. There was Alliance Bank Company, Vales Drug Store, The Great Atlantic and Pacific Tea Company, and Zang's Jewelry Store which sponsored the community clock shown on the right. Alliance Historical Society Collection

A typical window display during the 1920s at Geiger's Mens Store on Main Street in Alliance shows off the many straw hats available to their customers. Prices ranged from $1.95 to $5.86. Alliance Historical Society Collection

Above: The Lamborn Floral Company in Alliance, circa 19: Stark County Historical Society

Left: For a short time in the late 1920s the Stern and Mann Company operated a store in downtown Alliance. Located 353 East Main Street, its doors opened on November 30, 1929, in a building that one newspaper described as "the latest of modern styles." This photo shows the building o opening day. Despite its striking appearance, indirect lighting, pearl colored paneling, and luxurious carpeting, the store remained open for less than two years. Alliance Historical Society Collection

Republic Steel Blast Furnace, circa 1940. Karl Harsh Collection

Located on Fourth Street Northwest in Canton, this is the original Lang Monument Company building shown in 1927. They have since expanded considerably. They were founded in 1894. Lang Collection

The Halle Company of Cleveland built the Halle Brothers Store on North Market in 1930. *Repository* Files Collection

The Massillon Agathon Baseball Team, shown in 1920, were the Semi-Pro Champions of the United States. Massillon Museum Collection

Left: The Canton Car Company was the manufacturer of Hopper Cars for the W&LE Railroad during the Depression. Located at Mulberry and Fourth Street Southeast, this picture was taken during the 1930s. They are also proudly displaying N.R.A. signs, which stood for National Recovery Act, one of President Franklin D. Roosevelt's reforms during hard times. CC&S Railway Club Collection

Right: Downtown Massillon, circa 1928. Massillon Museum Collection

This Stark Electric Railroad car is about to make a turn on Market Street in Canton at Square, June 10, 1935. Bill Haldi Collection

The Avalon as a small custard stand and sandwich shop in 1935.
It was located on Cleveland Avenue North just north of Thirtieth
Street in Canton. *Repository* Files Collection

Left: Construction of First National Bank Building 1921, now
Bank One, replaced the Eagle Block at Tuscarawas and Market.
Repository Files Collection

The Avalon Drive-In in the 1950s was at the height of its popularity. It was a favorite watering spot of many teenagers. It closed in the early 1970s to make way for Wendy's Restaurant. *Repository* Files Collection

Right: The *Alliance Review* Building, built in 1901, is shown here February 5, 1931. The paper has been in existence since September 17, 1888. The ownership remained with the Hoiles/Peterson family until it was sold in the 1980s to Dix Publishing. This building was torn down in the 1970s. Alliance Historical Society Collection.

Top Facing Page: A busy day in downtown Alliance during the Roaring Twenties (looking east near Mechanic Street). Some of the popular stores during that period were The Boston Store, I.G.A. Grocery Store, and McCrory's. Alliance Historical Society Collection

The Spring and Holzwarth Company was one of the most popular stores in downtown Alliance. Commonly referred to as "The Big Store" it will always be remembered for the great fire that destroyed it in January 1931. They rebuilt and were later purchased by the M. O'Neil Company of Akron. They remained in business until the early 1970s. Alliance Historical Society Collection

The ladies clothing department at the Spring and Holzwarth Department Store in Alliance, circa 1920. Alliance Historical Society

The milk delivery men of the Hol-Guerns Dairy Company pose by their trucks outside the dairy plant on Cleveland Avenue prior to the 1941 expansion project. Hol-Guerns was the first area dairy to make use of tank trucks in bulk transportation of milk from local farms to the processing plant. Milk and Honey Collection

Left: The Fort Knight Men's Club of Massillon, shown here about 1935, was a social and civic organization in the '30s which focused on community concerns. They worked hand in hand with the Massillon Urban League. Marva Dotson Collection

Right: Shown here is the first milk wagon of the Hol-Guerns Dairy Company, founded by Francis X. Meyer in Canton. He established his first route in 1913 and in 1924 purchased seven Holstein and five Guernsey cows and the trade name Hol-Guerns Dairy was born. Meyer built his plant and dairy store at 3400 Cleveland Avenue Northwest in 1928 and made a $90,000 expansion in 1941. The dairy operated until 1969 when Superior Dairy acquired the routes. Milk and Honey Collection

Above: The McKinley Memorial Association Trustees around 1930 included, in the top row from left to right: Herbert Hoover, Sr., and Harry Ross Jones. In the middle row: James K. Lynch, Paul Belden, David D. Day, E. A. Langenbach, and Judge Henry W. Harter, Sr. In the front row left to right: H. H. Timken, George B. Cortelyou, Atlee Pomerene, unknown, and Austin Lynch. *Repository* Files Collection

Left: "Bank Night" drawing at the Louis Theater. This theater was operated by Mr. and Mrs. Wayne Kimball from 1935 to 1947. To promote attendance there was a weekly drawing for cash prizes. The participants had to be present to claim a prize, hence the crowd. The starting prize was $25.00 and as the pot built up to $100.00 a second drawing was inaugurated. Louisville Public Library Collection

National Guard Armory built in 1926. Located at Schroyer
Avenue Southwest Repository Files

These 1938–39 sophomore boys from Lincoln High School
show some independence by referring to themselves as the
MOB, probably room number 101. In the first row from left
right are: Don Huntley, Gene Loveless, Paul DeGarmo, Owe
Bing, A. J. Spivey, George Marx, Carl Dittmar, Jr., and Sam
Lemmo. In the second row are: Professor Richey, Allen
Smith, Elmer Mashek, Jack Skala, Jim Wilson, Bob Bonar,
Jim Richards, Ray Hooper. In the third row are: Glenn, Bob
Harris, Bob Shaffner, Don Curtis, Jim Ranier, Chuck Schlar
Jim Staudt, and Wally Mohr. In the fourth row are: J.
Anderson, Jim Betz, Kirk Foster, Chuch Bungard, Neil Rub
Jack Chabek, and Joe DeOrio. In the fifth row are: Jim
Ecrement, Don Sharp, Alfy Keeler, Jim Maullar, Earl Stock,
and Chuck Buker. Norma Boscia Collection

Architects H. L. Stevens and Company's rendering of the Hotel
Onesto on the corner of Cleveland Avenue and Second Street
Northwest. *Repository* Files Collection

A group of bandsmen pose with the Alliance Aerial Taxi plane in the 1920s. Alliance Historical Society Collection

Navarre band in the 1930s. Navarre Bethlehem Historical Society Collection

The Lembright Bakery was founded in 1907 by D. Fred Lembright and was located on Market Street. This photo shows the delivery trucks in front of the Lembright residence on East Milton in the late 1930s. Alliance Historical Society Collection

The northside of the 400 block of Main Street in the 1920s included Victoria Restaurant, F. W. Woolworth and Company, and Koch's Clothing Store. Alliance Historical Society Collection

The old Broad Avenue flying field in Canton in the 1920s.
Repository Files Collection

The African American First Baptist Church at Aultman (near
Greentown) was photographed about 1938. Emaline Turpin
Collection

J. C. Penney Co. opened in 1934 in downtown Canton at 201
Market Avenue and then moved to Mellett Mall in 1965. It was
reportedly the largest Penney's store in the nation at that time.
Marcella Emmons Collection

One of Waltz The Camera Man's first delivery trucks was
photographed in 1934. A strong believer in advertising and
service, Waltz grew to become one of Ohio's largest photo
finishers. *Repository* Files Collection

Shown here is a wrecked car on Shorb Avenue in Canton being towed away by Dunlap Towing Service. Dunlap was the first towing business in Canton, founded in 1926. Bruce Dunlap Collection

Children take a spin on a ride at Meyers Lake Park circa 1938. Nancy LePar Collection

George Herman Johnson—a "self-made" poet, dancer, producer, director, actor, and playwright—started the Negro Little Theatre at Massillon. In all he developed forty-eight productions and wrote a volume of two hundred poems all entitled "Why." Marva Dotson Collection

This building was originally constructed by *The Repository* in 1891 at Third and Market North in Canton. It became McCrory's in 1927. *Repository* Files Collection

The Massillon Negro Baseball League gathers at the corner of Erie Street and Tremont Southwest in Massillon. They are standing in front of the Boston Lunch, the Irwin Bar, and the Massillon Pool Room about 1935. Marva Dotson Collection

The Oscar Ritchie chorus, shown here about 1935, was directed by Dr. Oscar W. Ritchie, a professor at Kent State University and the first African American to serve on any Ohio University staff. Pictured in row one from left to right are: Mary Ballinger, Helen Brooks, Inez Ballinger, Mary Bell Johnson, Evelyn Adams, and Clentonia Provitt. In row two are: Dr. Oscar W. Ritchie, Edith Ritchie, Irene Brooks, Anna Coleman, Inez Johnson, Mrs. Montgomery, Eleanor Johnson, Ella Hobbs, Edna Grant, Mildred Gordon, and James Wardlaw. In row three are: Edgar Herring, Theodore Toles, Arvie Autrey, and Ray Myers. In row four are: Art Coleman, unknown, George Allen, Alex Woods, Freddie Bray, Clyde Brown, and Eugene Johnson. Marva Dotson Collection

The Haines Motor Car Company was located on the southwest corner of Arch and Prospect Streets. This photo was taken in the early 1930s. Alliance Historical Society Collection

Children gather at the Massillon Urban League on opening day,
May 19, 1936. Marva Dotson Collection

The Works Progress Administration provided long-range work relief for over four million jobless Americans from 1935 to 1936. WPA workers labored at such tasks as building schools, parks, roads, and other projects for civic improvement. Shown here are women on a sewing assembly line in Massillon. Marva Dotson Collection

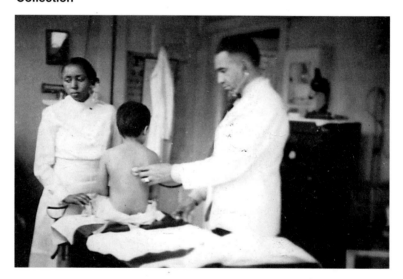

A Massillon physician, Dr. William B. Malloy, is shown here examining a young patient. Malloy practiced from 1923 to 1977 in Massillon. He is shown here with nurse Gerotha McGowan, R.N. She was the first African American registered nurse in Massillon. Marva Dotson Collection

Massillon State Hospital's first McKinley Hall was built in 1901, and dedicated three months after President McKinley's assassination. It contained an auditorium capable of seating eleven hundred people, library, lecture room, bowling alleys, and eighteen rooms for female employees and nurses. Yost and Packards were the architects. It burned down in the early 1930s. Stark County Historical Society Collection

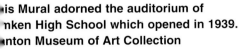

is Mural adorned the auditorium of nken High School which opened in 1939. nton Museum of Art Collection

ght: Lawyer Frank Bean, shown here in 30, practiced law in Canton. Martha tson Collection

The African American Luncheon Club, shown here around 1938, met on Wednesdays at the Phyllis Wheatly building. Heritage Information Center Collection, African American Research Committee

Central YMCA downstairs bowling alley in the 1930s.

Left: The early part of Thomas W. Cope's career included working as a furnace man, carpet salesman, and floor covering dealer. He was the first man in Alliance to rent and sell Hoover sweepers and to deal principally in rugs, carpets, and linoleum. In 1920 Cope bought out Cassaday and Pettit furniture business and moved into the Cassaday Building at 314 East Main Street where he remained until 1930. This photo shows the store during its Spring opening in March 1925. Alliance Historical Society Collection

The Esther Harkins Baby Orchestra made its debut in 1938 and performed over sixty concerts through the mid-1940s. Harkins, who organized the group, operated music studios in Louisville, Alliance, Salem, and Canton. She taught music in the North Canton Schools and was a charter member and first violinist with the Canton Symphony Orchestra. Pictured from left to right are: Ogereta Shreve, Joann Bolster, Susan Van Almen, Bradley Bolster, Evelyn Marie Huth, Richard Whiteleather, Carol Lebeau Whiteleather, Marilyn Jeannne Deckerd, Jerry Bledsoe, Mary Menges, Hohnny Polinori, Ruth Ann Clark, Sally Yarger, Cecelia Stoliper, Mary Ellen Clark, Frances Faunniel Clarke, and Nancy Stelts. Craig Bara Collection

WORLD WAR II
AND THE FUTURE

1940-1955

Even before the United States entered the war in 1941, many of the nation's industries, including those in Stark County, were making products through the Lend-Lease Program, initiated in 1939. Just before that in 1940, Mr. H. W. Hoover Sr., of the Hoover Company, sponsored seventy-four children of employees of the Hoover Limited plants in Great Britain, to come to Stark County "for the duration." They arrived in August and stayed in the area until 1945.

Along with the war contracts, that all the local steel companies had, a Naval Ordnance plant was built in Canton. Thousands of local young men and women joined the ranks of the armed forces. Those at home had to endure rationing, which included gasoline, meat, and sugar. A system of stamps was created and a Ration Board was organized to oversee the process of giving out the stamps.

War Bonds were "the" investment in those days and school children were organized to purchase saving stamps in booklets. The mails were censored and something called V-Mail was created to make mail loads lighter. It was a piece of stationery which carried the message, and then when properly folded became its own envelope.

Patriotism was at an all-time high during the early forties. President Franklin Roosevelt held regular radio talks with the nation at what were called "Fireside Chats." The movie houses carried news of the war and Hollywood provided numerous films about the war, such as *Best Years of our Lives, Guadalcanal Diary,*

Looking south on Market Street from Third Street toward the square in Downtown Canton, post-World War II, circa 1945. *Repository* Files Collection

Right: In 1958 the St. Haralambos Greek Congregation moved its church building from the southeast corner of Walnut and Sixth Street Southeast to Twenty-fifth Street Northwest. It is shown here moving through the square in Canton. Power lines had to be moved and traffic rerouted as the building inched its way north in two sections. When it was situated on the new site, the two sections were joined with a new part in the middle, thus providing an enlarged church. Marcella Emmons Collection

Clearing area around Timken Mercy Hospital for parking lot,
circa 1957. Nancy LePar Collection

Halloween on the square of Uniontown, circa 1950. May Parson
Collection

Mrs. Miniver, and the musical *Thank Your Lucky Stars.* Even the music of the day reflected a nation at war with songs such as "Rosie the Riveter," "Don't Sit Under the Apple Tree," and "White Cliffs of Dover."

After the war was over in 1945, many improvements happened in Stark County. In education, St. John's School for Boys merged with Mount Marie School for Girls and created Central Catholic High School. In fact, at this time a number of local public schools were consolidating to improve the education of the growing student population. Larger schools were built and curriculums improved. In 1957 Malone College opened in Canton. Stark Technical College and Walsh College were founded in 1960.

The circus comes to town at the Old Golf Links on the west side of Massillon about 1955. The photographer was John Coyne and the young boy is his son William Coyne who would lose his life in Vietnam. Massillon Museum Collection

In downtown Canton, this is the east side of Market Avenue looking north at Second and Tuscarawas Streets, circa 1947. Marcella Emmons Collection

Roadways improved significantly. In 1957 ground breaking for Interstate 77 was held. With a progressive roadway system backed by still active railroads, a successful trucking industry became part of our Stark County heritage.

In keeping with the growing patterns of many American communities, an airport was built. The first flight from Akron-Canton Regional Airport was on July 1, 1948. The facility rests on the Stark and Summit counties border.

The great urban industrial age was followed by a period of suburbanization which has been characterized by a change from "industrial" to a "service" economy and by the shifting of population and businesses from the downtown areas to the suburbs. These changes have mainly occurred since World War II and took place across the nation. While industries are certainly still

In 1941 Frederick W. Preyer purchased the Case property on Market Avenue North. He gave the house to the Art Institute and rented the garage to the Player's Guild for $1.00 a year. *Repository* Files Collection

This is downtown Canton, the east side of Market and Fourth Street looking north, circa 1956. Marcella Emmons Collection

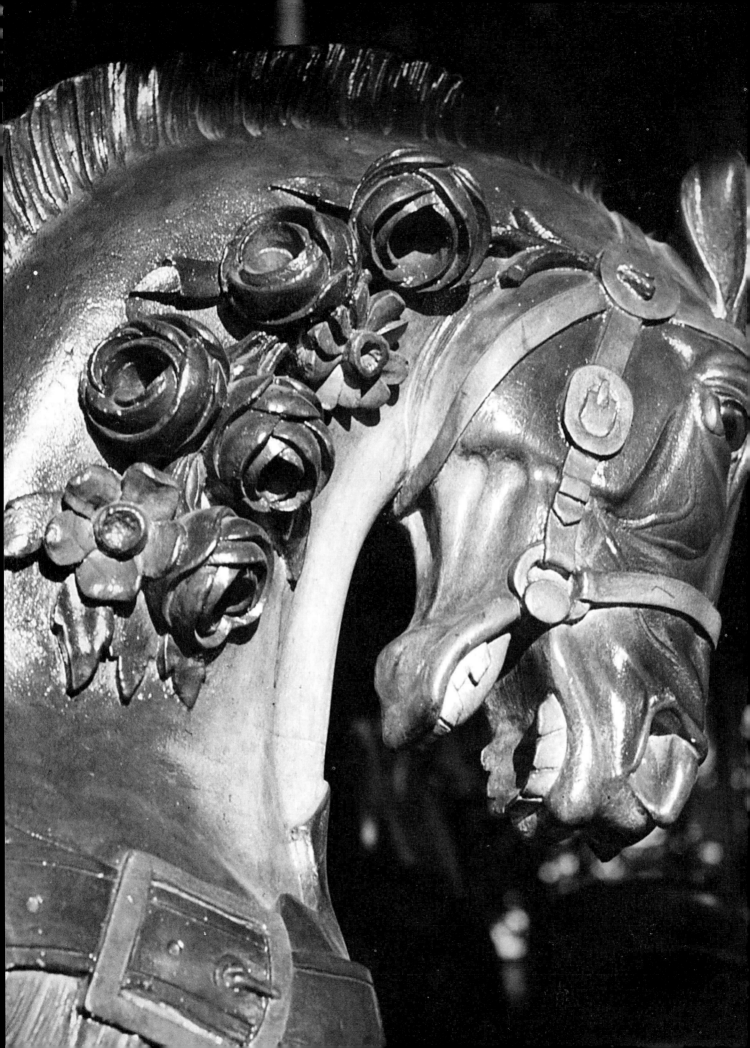

North Canton Hospital was operated by Mrs. Samuel Painter. It stood where the Society Bank now stands at North Main and Tenth Street. *Repository* Files Collection

Left: Close-up of carved horse head at Meyers Lake Park Carousel, circa 1947. Marcella Emmons Collection

located in Stark County, the area has followed a national trend toward service industries which are described as including banking and finance, retailing, insurance, medicine, law, and government, thus moving away from manufacturing.

The service economy has influenced the shift from the cities to the suburbs. In the 1950s four shopping plazas were built and would be followed by Belden Village in 1970. These and many other shopping complexes have drawn businesses away from downtown areas. Population is also growing more rapidly in suburban areas because of the powerful advancement of housing, which is being done on sections of land that were farms when Stark County was still young. Notable expansion has occurred in Jackson Township and North Canton. Churches and especially schools, still focal points of the communities, are struggling to adjust to this rapid population shift.

In 1955 Canton observed its Sesquicentennial—one hundred fifty years of being the center of the spiritual, educational, social, and political happenings. There will be changes and new challenges to keep the communities alive and productive as Stark County heads for its Bicentennial in 2009.

The Christmas tree in downtown Canton was set in the middle of Market Avenue from Third Street Southwest, circa 1945. Marcella Emmons Collection

This aerial view of downtown Massillon shows the flood control
project and straightening of river, circa 1940. Massillon Museum
Collection

Howard D. Miller Post No. 436 of the American Legion met in this
building located one mile south of the Uniontown Square on the
west side of Cleveland Avenue. This building was originally
constructed in 1920 and served over the years as a nightclub
and restaurant. The Legion bought it in 1946 and it was razed on
May 21, 1967, by area firemen in a training session. May Parsons
Collection

The Fairmount Children's Home Band, shown here in 1946, played in local parades and for the students that lived at Fairmount. Carol Freday Collection

Gathering for mass at St. Joseph's Catholic Church on West Tuscarawas Street in Canton. Marcella Emmons Collection

Homes located on Fifteenth Street Southwest in Canton were damaged by the tornado of August 13, 1943. Karl Harsh Collection

In 1931 the YWCA bought the old Judge Underhill residence in Canton, which was owned before that by Judge George Raff, first judge of Stark County's Probate Court back in 1856. The YWCA occupied this building until 1951. *Repository* Files Collection

Canton's Sesquicentennial Queen's Court in 1955. Delores Boyajian Collection

S. S. Kresge Company in downtown Canton during the early
1950s. *Repository* File Collection

Looking south along Market Avenue North. The Finney
drugstores were first established in 1899. W. T. Grant Company
is under construction in this circa 1954 photograph. Marcella
Emmons Collection

View of Canton City Hall and Safety Building, circa 1959.
Marcella Emmons Collection

Post-World War II parade in downtown Canton, circa 1945.
Joanne Poole Collection

Left: Christmas 1960 on the square in downtown Canton.
***Repository* Files Collection**

Left: Herbert W. Hoover replaced his father "Boss" Hoover as president of the Hoover Company. Hoover Files

Right: "Boss" William H. Hoover, founder of the Hoover Leather Factory and Hoover Suction Sweeper Company. Hoover Company Files

Clarence Thomas, former Canton Urban League Director. Urban League Files

Right: Be sure to eat at "Kresge's Canteen" where lemonade was 5¢ and a peach banana split cost you 15¢. This picture was taken on August 10, 1942. Alliance Historical Society Collection

Seen here is Mr. Herbert W. Hoover, Jr., then president of the
Hoover Company and grandson of W. H. "Boss" Hoover. He is
conferring with executives from the Canadian plant. Pictured
from left to right are: Walter A. Munz, T. O. Watts, and R. L.
Winegard. *Repository* Files Collection

Moonlight Ballroom, Meyers Lake Park, circa 1950. *Repository* **Files Collection**

Gordon Price, one of the founders of the Art Institute, now Canton Museum of Art, works at his desk in the Little Civic Art Gallery. Canton Museum of Art Collection

National Fireproof Company round-house at Aultman, near Greentown, circa 1940. Emaline Turpin Collection

This 1948 photo shows the F. E. Brechbuhler and Sons Scale Sales and Service at their 4704 Wiseland Avenue Southeast North Industry location. From left to right are: Bud Bagent, F. E. Brechbuhler, Wayne E. Brechbuhler, and Clyde B. Brechbuhler. Brechbuhler Collection

This view of downtown Canton, the east side of Market Avenue North, between Fifth and Sixth Streets, looks north about 1947. The magnificent Loew's Theater was opened February 9, 1927. It was the first Loew's built outside Cleveland. Marcella Emmons Collection

Canton Police Boys Club perform at the Onesto Hotel under the direction of Walter Crenshaw, accompanied by Marion Crenshaw, circa 1940. Crenshaw Collection

Menelik Cultural Club gathers for their annual Garden Party at the home of Dr. and Mrs. M. B. Williams, circa 1940. Crenshaw Collection

Dr. Raymond James Ballinger (1902–1979) was a longtime physician in Massillon, practicing from 1931 to 1979. Marva Dotson Collection

MASTER CHRONOLOGY OF STARK COUNTY, OHIO

1805-1955

Note: All population figures are for Stark County.

1787	July 13	Northwest Ordinance enacted by U.S. Congress
	September 17	**United States Constitution signed**
1803	March 1	Ohio admitted to the Union as the seventeenth state.
1805	May 14	Bezaleel Wells buys land (566 square miles, part of which becomes Canton) from U.S. Government at $2.00 per acre.
	July 4	Treaty of Fort Industry opens lands west of the Tuscarawas River for settlement.
	November 15	Village of Canton founded by Bezaleel Wells. Original plat recorded for Canton at Liston-then county seat.
1806	January 27	Ohio General Assembly passes act to build State Road from New Lisbon to Tuscarawas River, part of which is not the Lincoln Highway; first road in Canton.
	May 14	Village of Osnaburg founded (renamed East Canton 1918).
	October 6	Village of Bethlehem founded.
	October 22	Horse races were held at the fork of Nimishillen south of Canton, to sell Canton lots.
		First gristmill in Canton built by Phillip. Slusser.
1807	March 7	Village of Lexington founded.
		First store opened by John Shorb (Canton).
1809	March 16	Stark County founded, five townships established-Canton, Plain, Nimishillen, Osnaburg, and Sandy.
	April 3	First County elections held.
		Canton began as county seat; post office opened.
		(1810 population: 2,734)
1810	March 5	Tuscarawas Township formed from Canton Township.
		First church built in Canton. (Reformed/Lutheran).
1811		Thomas Rotch brings Merino sheep to Stark County to raise (Massillon area).
1812-14		**War of 1812 fought with Great Britain.**
1812	April 20	Village of Kendal founded (became Massillon 1826).
1813	December 7	Perry Township formed from Canton Township.
		First brickyards started.
1814	January 14	Village of Waynesburg founded.
	January 14	Village of Paris founded.

	March 23	Village of Milan founded (became part of Canal Fulton).
1815	March 6	Pike Township formed from Canton Township.
	March 22	Village of Sparta (East Sparta) founded.
	March 30	*Ohio Repository* newspaper founded in Canton.
	April 1	Jackson Township formed from Plain Township.
	December 4	Lawrence Township formed from Plain Township.
	September 2	First Trading Company (Farmers & Mechanics Trading Company).
	April 25	First in Canton, Farmer's Bank, opens.
		John Shorb, President; William Fogle, Cashier.
		Bridges built over East and West branches of the Nimishillen.
1816	February 6	Village of Greentown founded (originally called Green).
	March 4	Lexington Township formed from Nimishillen Township.
	March 4	Sugar Creek Township formed from Canton Township.
	April 9	Village of Uniontown founded.
	June 4	Bethlehem Township formed from Canton Township.
	December 12	Lake Township formed from Plain Township.
	November 23	Canton Library Company, a subscription library, founded.
1817		Bezaleel Wells sells 1,080 acres of land around Wells Lake to Andrew Meyer, which became Meyers Lake.
		Wells Lake renamed Meyers Lake.
		First Catholic Mass held at John Shorb's farm.
1818	April 1	Paris Township formed from Osnaburg Township.
		Stark County's first courthouse completed.
		(1820 population: 12,406)
1821	March 1	Canton Masonic Lodge No. 69 F.&A.M. organized.
	December 3	Washington Township formed from Lexington Township.
		Marlboro Township formed from Lexington Township.
		Original Presbyterian church organized in Canton.
1822	January 30	Canton incorporated as a village.
	May 8	General John Stark dies in Manchester, N.H.
		First Fire Department established (Canton).
1824		First Catholic church in Canton built, (St. John the Baptist).
		Charity Rotch school opens in Kendal.
1825		First stagecoach line from Canton (Henry Barber).
1826	November 24	Village of Massillon, formerly Kendal, founded.
		Village of Fulton founded (became part of Canal Fulton, 1853)
1827	April 3	Village of Williamsport founded (became part of Alliance, 1850).
	November 14	Village of Marlboro founded.
	November 28	Village of Harrisburg founded.
1828		Ohio Canal built to Massillon. Full route was from Cleveland to Portsmouth.
1829	June 13	Village of McDonaldsville founded.
	June 16	Village of East Greenville founded.
		(1830 population: 26,558)
1830	June 22	Village of Lima founded (became Limaville in 1838).
1831	January 25	Village of New Franklin founded (originally Franklin).
	February 19	Village of New Berlin founded (renamed North Canton, 1918).
	May 10	Village of West Massillon founded.
	August 27	Village of New Baltimore founded.
1832		Ohio and Erie Canal completed (Cleveland to Portsmouth)).
1833	June 5	Village of Minerva founded.

	August 22	Village of Mount Union founded. (incorporated into Alliance 1888).
	October 18	Village of Rochester founded (incorporated into Navarre, 1871).
		Stark County Democrat newspaper founded.
1834	March 24	Village of Navarre founded.
	April 26	Village of Magnolia founded.
	October 8	Village of Louisville founded.
1836	May 20	Village of Milton founded (renamed Wilmot, 1850).
	June 18	Village of Richville founded.
		Joshua Gibbs patents plow.
1837		Stark County Infirmary built.
1838	July 31	Village of Freedom founded (became part of Alliance, 1850).
		Canton incorporated as a town (John Meyers elected first Mayor).
		Massillon incorporated as a town (repealed, 1845).
		(1840 population: 34,603)
1841	November 26	Village of Robertsville founded.
1842	January 1	C. M. Russell & Company founded.
	February 26	Village of Freeburg founded.
	April 6	Village of Mapleton founded.
	August 17	Village of Maximo founded (originally Strasburg).
1845		St. Peter's Catholic Church organized.
	June 9	First Odd Fellows Lodge organized.
1846	October 20	Mount Union subscription school founded.
1848		Massillon Public Schools established.
1849		Village of Belfort founded.
		Mount Union subscription school becomes Mount Union Seminary.
		Canton Public School System started by Ira Allen.
		(1850 population: 39,878)
1850	September 26	Alliance founded, combining villages of Freedom, Liberty, and Williamsport.
	Oct. 15-16	First Stark County Fair held.
		Village of Milton is renamed Wilmot.
1851	October 2	Village of Cairo founded.
		Village of Hartville founded.
		C. Aultman and Company begins manufacturing reapers and mowers in Greentown then moves to Canton.
		Cleveland and Pittsburgh Railroad completed through Alliance.
1852		Pennsylvania and Ohio Railroad opens through Canton.
1853		Villages of Milan and Fulton combine to form Canal Fulton.
		Massillon incorporated as a village.
1854		Canton incorporated as City (B. F. Leiter elected first Mayor).
		Alliance incorporated as a village.
		Isaac Harter and Sons Bank founded (evolved to United National Bank).
1855		Deuble Jewelry Store opened.
1857	November 3	Village of North Lawrence founded.
1858		Mount Union Seminary becomes Mount Union College.
1859	June 4-5	Late frost kills spring crops in all of Northeastern Ohio.
		(1860 population: 42,978)
1861-65		**U.S. Civil War fought.**
1863		First National Bank of Canton founded (became Central Trust in 1975).
		Massillon Independent Newspaper founded.
1864		Bucher and Gibbs Plow Company opened.

1866	April 16	Canton YMCA founded. (reorganized, 1886).
1867		William McKinley begins to practice law in Canton.
		Issac Harter Private Bank founded (became First Savings then Canton National Bank, then United Bank).
1868		Opera House built in Canton (second in Ohio)
		Massillon incorporated as a city.
		Canton Fire Department buys first steam engine.
1869		Wrought Iron Bridge Company built.
		Smith-Trump Abstract Company founded.
		(1870 population: 52,508)
1870	February 22	Second Stark County Courthouse dedicated.
		C. N. Vicary Clothing Store opened.
1871	August 29	Village of Navarre incorporated, combining Bethlehem, Rochester, and early Navarre.
	August	Morgan Engineering Company moves to Alliance from Pittsburgh.
1872	March 5	Village of Beach City founded.
		Diebold Manufacturing moves to Canton from Cincinnati.
		Yohe Supply Company founded.
1874	June 5	Village of Justus founded.
		Iron Moulders Union Beneficial Association organized (first union in the area)
		Dumonts Sporting Goods Store opened.
1875		W. H. Hoover Company begins manufacture of leather horse gear in New Berlin.
		H.S. Belden began manufacture of brick.
1876		Canton Business College founded.
		William McKinley elected to Congress.
	November 1	Fairmount Children's Home established.
1877		Muck farming begins at Hartville swamps.
1878		*Repository* begins daily publication.
		Canton Steel Company begins operations.
		Thurin's Furniture Store opened.
1879		Ney Manufacturing Company founded.
		(1880 population: 63,031)
1880	January 20	Valley Railroad completed from Cleveland to Canton.
	May 11	First telephone switchboard installed in Canton.
	May 15	Connotton Valley Railroad built to Canton.
	December 12	First telephone switchboard installed in Massillon.
1881	September 12	Village of Middlebranch founded.
		Telephones installed in Alliance.
1882	June 21	Village of Howenstine founded.
		Canton Car Company organized.
1883		Deuble's Jewelry Store opened.
		Dumont's Seed Company founded.
		McKenzie and Jones Clothing Store opened.
1884		Canton Citadel of the Salvation Army founded.
		Canton Street Railway Company founded using horse-drawn streetcars.
1885		Massillon Citadel of the Salvation Army founded.
		Canton Public Library Association formed.
		Temple Israel congregation organized.

		Canton City Hall replaced.
		Belden Brick company organized.
	December	Canton Board of Trade organized.
1886	October	Alliance Citadel of the Salvation Army founded.
		Canton YMCA permanently reorganized.
		Canton Electric Light and Power Company reorganized.
		Berger Manufacturing Company established (becomes part of Republic Steel, 1930).
		Agudas Achim Synagogue organized.
		Cummins Storage Company organized.
1886-1888		Dueber-Hampden Watch Works factory erected (razed in 1958).
1887		Association of Charities founded (renamed Family Service).
		Louisville Herald newspaper founded.
		Electric power available in Canton.
		First paved road in Canton.
		Home Savings and Loan founded (for many years First Federal, became First American, FSB in 1987).
		Canton Hardware Wholesale Company founded.
		Stern and Mann Clothing Store founded.
		News Depot opened.
		Canton Flower Shop founded.
		Professional Football Organized in Canton.
1888		*Alliance Review* newspaper founded.
		Canton Steel Roofing Company opened.
		Troy Laundry Company opened.
1889		Schumacher Lumber founded (Hartville).
		Electric power available in Massillon.
		Canton Supply Company founded.
		Furbay Electric Company founded.
		(1890 population: 84,170)
1890	December 12	First YMCA building in Stark County opens in Canton.
		St. Paul's African Methodist Episcopal church organized in Canton.
		First National Bank of Massillon founded.
1891	May 20	Village of North Industry founded.
		Frankham Brass and Bronze Company founded.
		George D. Harter Bank incorporated as state bank.
		William McKinley elected governor of Ohio.
		Bonnot Company opened.
1892	January 11	McKinley inaugurated governor of Ohio.
	January 17	Aultman Hospital opens.
	March 31	Massillon State Hospital founded.
	July 2	East-west streetcar interurban line opens, Canton to Massillon.
		Stocker Cigar Store opened.
1893	May 23	Village of Reedurban founded.
		Third County Courthouse built by remodeling and enlarging the second building.
		J. B. McCoy Candy Company founded.
		McKinley re-elected governor of Ohio.
		Canton Actual Business College established.
1894	January 8	McKinley again inaugurated as governor.

		First Canton-Massillon high school football game.
		A group of steel men from Pennsylvania headed by William W. Irwin opened first rolling mill in Canton.
1895		Dime Savings Bank founded.
1896		Aultman Home for Aged Women opens.
	November 3	McKinley elected twenty-fifth president of U.S.
		Congress Lake Club founded.
		Shaeffer-Black Wholesale Food Distributors opens.
1897	March 4	McKinley inaugurated president.
	July 7	Canton Business and Canton Actual College merged.
1898		Weber Dental Manufacturing Company founded.
		Canton Iron and Metal Company founded. (evolved to Luntz Iron and Steel)
		Canton Rubber Company founded.
		Canton Attorney, William R. Day named secretary of state by President McKinley; later headed Peace Commission in Paris.
		Troy Laundry Company founded.
1899	January	Massillon Public Library opens
		Arnold Funeral Home established.
		Timken Roller Bearing and Axle Company moves to Canton from St. Louis.
		Finney's Drug Store opens.
		Citizens Building and Loan Company founded (becomes Citizens Savings Bank, in 1985; Citizens National Bank 1995).
		Canton Roll and Machine Company founded.
		Wagener Steam Pump Company organized.
		(1900 population: 94,747)
1900	November 6	McKinley re-elected president of U.S.
		Alliance City Hospital founded.
		C. A. Kolp Real Estate Company opened.
1901	May 15	North-south streetcar interurban opens, Cleveland to Canton.
	June 11	Canton's Central Labor Union organized.
	September 6	President McKinley shot by assassin Leon Czolgosz in Buffalo, N.Y.
	September 14	President McKinley dies in Buffalo.
		Alliance Manufacturing Company founded.
		Canton Stamp and Enameling Company established.
		Timken Roller Bearing Company moved to Canton from St. Louis.
1902		Metropolitan Paving Brick Company incorporated (largest paving brick manufacturer in world).
		Eynon Plumbing Company incorporated.
1903	June 23	McCaskey Register Company (Alliance) Incorporated.
		Electric power available in Louisville.
		Canton Symphony founded.
		Canton Drop Forging and Manufacturing Company opens.
		William R. Day of Canton appointed justice of the U.S. Supreme Court.
1904		Alliance Public Library opens.
		Canton City Auditorium built (razed, 1956).
1905		Visiting Nurse Society founded.
		Massillon City Hospital founded.
		Lamborn Floral Company founded (Alliance).
		Mount Marie School for Girls Established.

		Leatherman's Seed Store opened.
		Hahn and Company Store opened (pianos and organs).
		First Amish/Mennonite families moved to Stark County, settling in Hartville.
1906		Village of Brewster founded.
		Union Metal Manufacturing Company founded.
		Republic Stamping and Enameling Company founded.
1907	September 30	McKinley National Memorial dedicated.
		Alfred Nickles Bakery founded in Navarre.
		First Commercial alloy steel poured in Canton at United Steel Company under direction of Henry Ford.
		Needlework Guild organized.
		T. K. Harris Agency opened.
		Canton Pressing Printing Company founded.
1908	August 8	Hoover Electric Suction Sweeper Company founded by W. H. Hoover Company (New Berlin).
		Electric power available in New Berlin.
		Schneider Lumber Company founded.
	September 24	Mercy Hospital opens (evolves to Timken Mercy Medical Center).
		Hygienic Products Company and Climalene Company entered soft water field.
1909		YWCA in Canton organized.
		Reserve Printing Company.
1909-11		Mercy Hospital was constructed next to McKinley home (north Market and Ninth Street).
		(1910 population: 122,987)
1910		Canton Automobile Club organized.
		Nusbaum Jewelry Store opened.
		Cowgill Flower Shop opened.
		Melbourne Brothers Construction Company founded.
1911		Mohler Lumber Company opened.
		Harrison Paint Company organized.
		Canton Real Estate Board organized.
1912		Stark Dry Goods founded (became M. O'Neil Company).
1914		Canton Chamber of Commerce founded.
	June	**World War I erupts in Europe.**
		Ewing Chevrolet Company opened.
		T. K. Harris Company founded.
		Canton Tire Service.
1915		First blast furnaces built.
		Hercules Motors Corporation (gas engines).
1916-18		First wing of McKinley High School built followed by second wing (1920-1921).
1916		Pennsylvania Railroad Station built in Canton (razed, 1976).
	June 29	YPCA (Young People's Christian Association) organized in Massillon.
1917		Canton Chapter of the American Red Cross founded.
		United States enters World War I.
		Ideal Furniture Store opened.
1918		New Berlin renamed North Canton.
		Osnaburg renamed East Canton.
	November 11	**World War I ends.**

		Canton McKinley High School built (9th Street at north Market).
		Mathie Building Supply Company opened.
		Eclipse Electric Fixture Company opened.
1919		Catholic Community League founded.
		Ohio Power Company formed from several smaller companies.
		Massillon YMCA founded.
		Superior Sheet Steel organized.
		McQueen Sign Company opened.
		Ohio Battery and Ignition Company founded.
		Ziegler Tire and Supply Store opened.
		(1920 population: 177,218)
1920		Goodwill Industries established.
		American Legion Post No. 44 founded in Canton.
		Canton Urban League organized.
		Stark Jewish News newspaper founded.
		Canton Woman's Club founded.
		Kramer Motor Company founded (Hudson dealer)
		Fleishour Shoe Store opened.
		Molly Stark Sanitorium.
1921		Massillon YWCA organized, YPCA dissolved.
		Boy Scout Council established (some troops predate council).
		Main headquarters for Ohio Power Company established in Canton.
		Home Savings and Loan organized.
1922		Canton Welfare Federation established (merged with United Way, 1984).
		Canton Community Chest established (became United Way in 1974).
		First school police in U.S. for directing traffic established at Canton's Worley school.
		North Canton Sun newspaper founded.
		Evans Realtor founded.
1923		Original Community Building-YMCA built in North Canton.
1924	March 24	Girl Scout Council organized (Canton area).
	July 7	First Girl Scout camp opens.
	October 20	Philamatheon Society for the Blind established.
		Canton Jewish Center organized.
		Construction of Masonic Temple in Canton begins.
		Ashland Oil Company Canton refinery opens.
		Republic Steel produces first stainless steel.
		Art's Jewelry Store opened.
		Franz-Royer Electric Company opened.
		Henry A. Zelinsky, Incorporated founded (demolition/wrecking).
		Buckeye Oxygen Company organized.
1925	February 13	WHBC radio station founded as church station for shut-ins.
	February 22	Massillon YMCA building dedicated.
		St. John's High School founded.
	November	People's Commerce and Loan Bank founded (evolved to Ameritrust, 1975).
1926	February 26	Alliance YWCA founded.
		William McKinley School of Law opens (closed, 1956).
		Palace Theatre built in Canton.
		Armory built (Shroyer Avenue S.W., Canton)
		Canton received automatic dial system of telephone service.

1927		Sugardale Foods, Incorporated founded.
		The Canton Repository bought by Brush-Moore newspapers, Incorporated Little Flower Hospital.
1928	May 29	Ohio Ferro Alloy Corporation established.
	June 20	Swiss Club organized.
		Tam O'Shanter golf course opens.
1929	August 10	Village of Hills and Dales incorporated.
		Molly Stark Hospital dedicated.
	October 29	**Stock market crashes; start of Great Depression.**
		Buxbaum Manufacturing Company (rubber products).
		Waltz-the-Camera Man opened.
		(1930 population: 221,784)
1930	August 20	Onesto Hotel opens in Canton.
		Republic Steel Corporation formed.
		Halle Brothers Department Store of Cleveland opened store in Canton.
		Brush-Moore Newspapers Incorporated purchased.
		Canton Daily News (The Repository becomes Canton's only daily).
		Timken locomotive, equipped with roller bearings placed into service.
1931		Peoples Bank established.
1932		Canton Players Guild founded.
		Matthews Funeral Home founded.
		Eaton Manufacturing founded (Massillon).
		Canton Economist (newspaper) founded.
		Office Equipment Company established.
		Lattavo Company organized (steel haulers).
		Canton Hardware Wholesale Company opened.
1933		Massillon Museum established.
1934		Canton Art Institute established (formerly Little Civic Art Gallery).
		Canton Jaycees organized.
		Flanagan and Nist Paint Store opened.
		Ross Independent Oil Company founded.
1935		Canton Music Association established.
1936		Canton Labor Union disbands; Canton Federation of Labor organized (affiliated with AF of L).
		Dunlap Towing Service founded.
		Louise Shop (ladies wear) opened.
		Canton's Park System completed (cost of $1 million dollars).
1937		Canton's Fawcett Stadium built.
	March 22	US Steel unionizes under CIO (Committee of Industrial Organization).
	April 16	Timken unionizes under CIO.
	May 26	Little Steel Strike begins; at least 12 killed during course of strike.
	June 23	Ohio National Guard called up.
	July 15	Strike ends.
1938	February 16	First performance of the newly organized Canton Symphony Orchestra Association was held at the city auditorium.
1939	September	Timken Vocational High School opens.
		Kempthorn Motors opens.
		Alliance Historical Society founded.
		Ohio Broadcasting Company (WHBC) erected studios and five-hundred-foot tower at South Market and Fifth Streets in Canton.

		Torrey Sub-Station erected by Ohio Power Company.
	September	**World War II begins in Europe.**
		(1940 population: 234,887)
1940		WHBC becomes an affiliate of the Mutual Broadcasting System.
1941-1947		Naval Ordnance plant in production.
1941	December 7	**Pearl Harbor bombed by Japan, U.S. enters World War II.**
1945		**War ends with Germany in May and with Japan in August.**
1946		St. John's High School and Mount Marie School for Girls merge to become Central Catholic High School.
		First motels open in Stark County (Chase, D and T, Paradise Court).
	October 4	Sancta Clarra Monastery dedicated.
		Stark County Historical Society founded.
		Arrowhead Country Club opens.
1947		Ford plant opens.
1948	July 1	First passenger flight from Akron-Canton airport.
		Little League baseball organized (first league west of the Alleghenies).
		Danner Press began operations.
		(1950 population 283,194)
1950		Field House opens (near Fawcett Stadium).
		Bliss Company, sheet metal fabricators, begins operation in former Ordnance plant.
		Stark County Times begins to publish.
1951		Canton Memorial Auditorium opens.
	July 17	Country Fair Shopping center opens.
		Canton YWCA opens new facility at Sixth and Walnut Streets N.E.
1952		Junior Achievement organized.
		McKinley Plaza Shopping Center opens.
		Salvation Army opens new facility.
		Ecko Products Company of Chicago purchased Republic Stamping and Enameling Company.
		United Way replaced Community Chest and Red Feather Organizations.
	February 4	Mercy Hospital opens satellite hospital in former Timken House in downtown.
1954	March 29	Amherst Park shopping center opens (Massillon).
1955		Mahoning Road Plaza shopping center opens. Canton Sesquicentennial celebrated.

INDEX

EPILOGUE

Our historical crystal ball tells us that the next period of time will bring enormous changes to Stark County. Kent State University will open a campus here in 1967, at the same time the local television station begins to operate. The professional Football Hall of Fame will open in 1963 and really put Stark County on the map. Doctors Osteopathic Hospital will be established in the same year in Perry Township.

Several strong local banks will merge with out-of-town banks, connecting us electronically with other parts of the state. The family owned Hoover Company will sell first to Chicago Pacific, but in a short time, Maytag will buy the sweeper company or "broom works" as it used to be called, and the Timken Company will build a computerized steel manufacturing facility called Faircrest.

The Canton City Auditorium will be built in conjunction with the magnificent Cultural Center, which will be made possible by the Timken and Hoover Foundations. The facility will house the Canton Museum of Art, Players Guild, Canton Symphony, Canton Civic Opera, and Canton Ballet.

Throughout its history, Stark County has taken advantage of its geographic location and natural resources to grow and prosper. The earliest settlers used the rich land to raise wheat and other crops for market. With transportation advantages provided by the Ohio and Erie Canal and the railroads, other resources like coal were used to build new industries. During the great steel age, industrial expansion and urbanization were joined by a growing interest in providing human services through charitable organizations. Finally, this period of urbanization has been followed by a time of suburbanization, as business and people move to the edges of the cities, a change which mirrors the national picture.

We have come a long way from Conestoga wagons to convertibles, from tin to plastic, from iron cookware to teflon, from paving bricks to concrete, from nickelodeons to television and videos, and from party lines to cellular phones. We have even developed an electronic super highway and have been to the moon. One can only guess what will be next.